A-Z ROYAL TUNB[RIDGE WELLS] SEVENOAKS

C000242497

CONTENTS

Key to Map Pages	Back Cover
Map Pages	2-39
Index to Villages, Hospitals and Selected Places of Interest	40-52

REFERENCE

Motorway	M25	Church or Chapel	†
A Road	A26	Cycleway	
Under Construction		Fire Station	■
Proposed		Hospital	Ⓗ
B Road	B2176	House Numbers (Selected roads)	145 / 98
Dual Carriageway		Information Centre	🄸
One-way Street — Traffic flow on A Roads is also indicated by a heavy line on the driver's left.	⇒ / ⇒	National Grid Reference	⁵65
Restricted Access		Police Station	▲
Pedestrianized Road		Post Office	★
Track / Footpath		Toilet:	
Residential Walkway		without facilities for the disabled	▽
Railway — Level Crossing / Station / Tunnel		with facilities for the disabled	▽
		for the disabled only	▽
Heritage Railway		Educational Establishment	
Built-up Area	QUEEN ST	Hospital or Health Centre	
Local Authority Boundary		Industrial Building	
Posttown Boundary		Leisure or Recreational Facility	
Postcode Boundary (within Posttown)		Place of Interest	
Map Continuation	5	Public Building	
		Shopping Centre & Market	
Car Park (Selected)	P	Other Selected Buildings	

Scale

1:19,000

0   ¼   ½   ¾ Mile

0   250   500   750 Metres   1 Kilometre

3⅓ inches (8.47 cm) to 1 mile

5.26 cm to 1 kilometre

Copyright of Geographers' A-Z Map Company Limited

Head Office :
Fairfield Road, Borough Green, Sevenoaks, Kent TN15 8PP
Tel: 01732 781000

www.a-zmaps.co.uk

Ordnance Survey® This product includes mapping data licensed from Ordnance Survey® with the permission of the Controller of Her Majesty's Stationery Office.

ⒸCrown Copyright 2003. Licence number 100017302

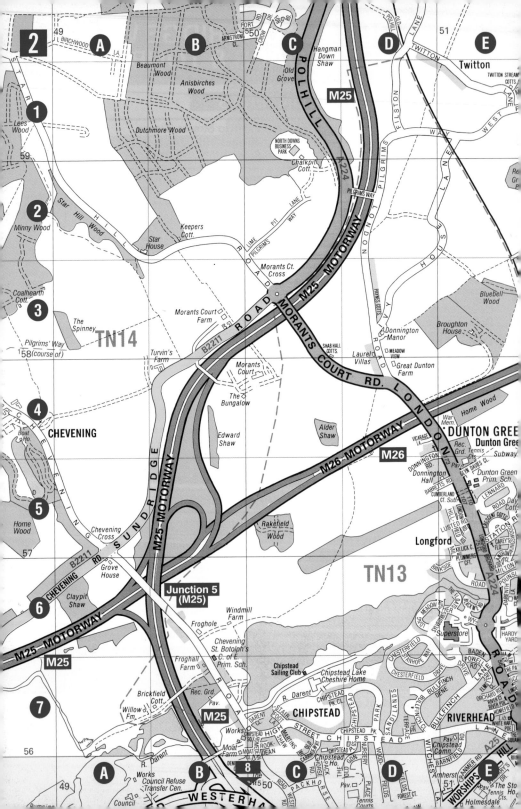

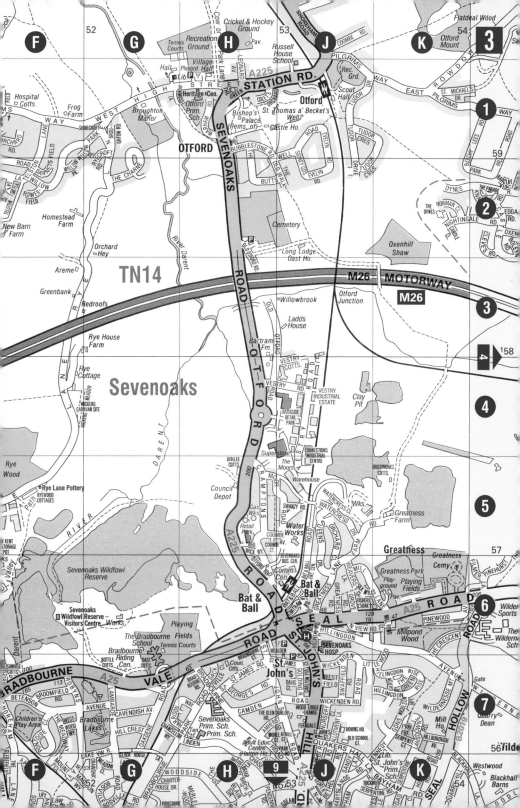

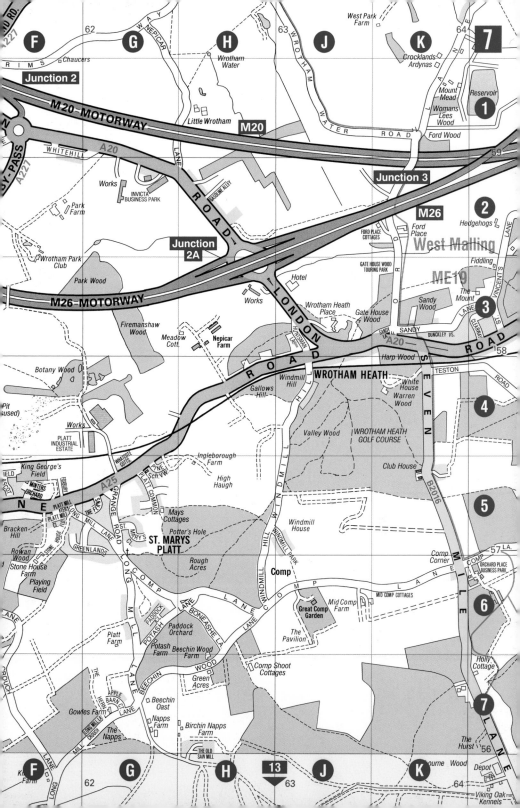

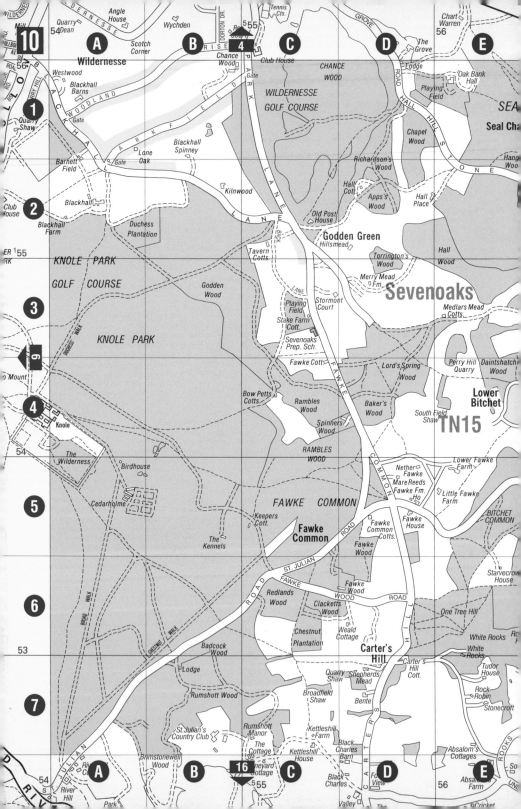

Sevenoaks

TN15

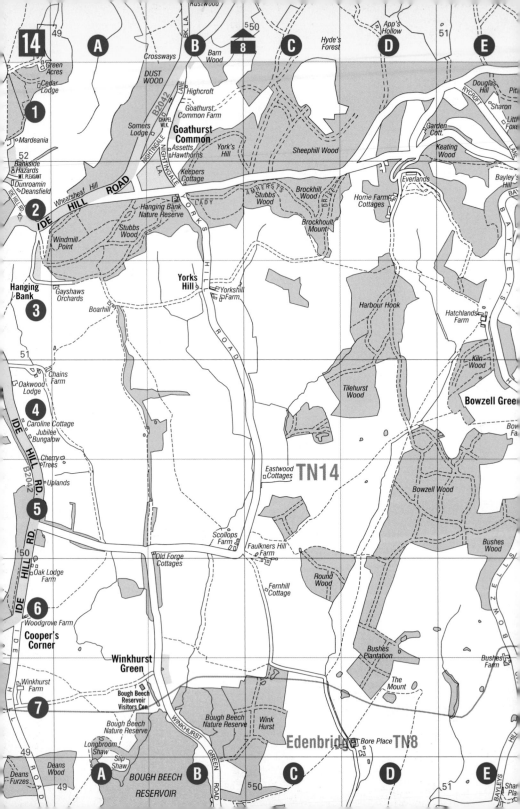

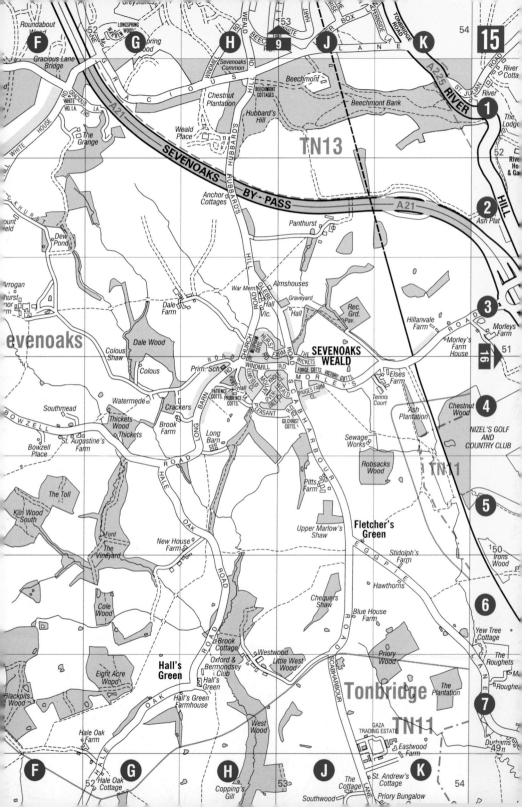

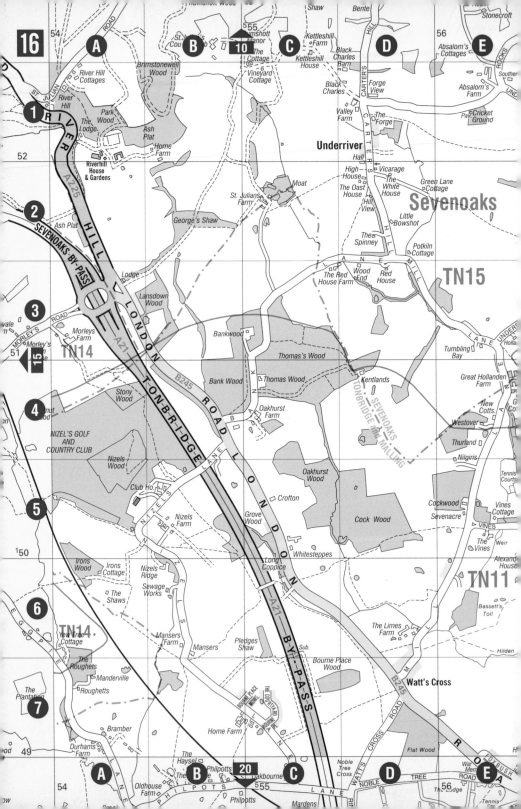

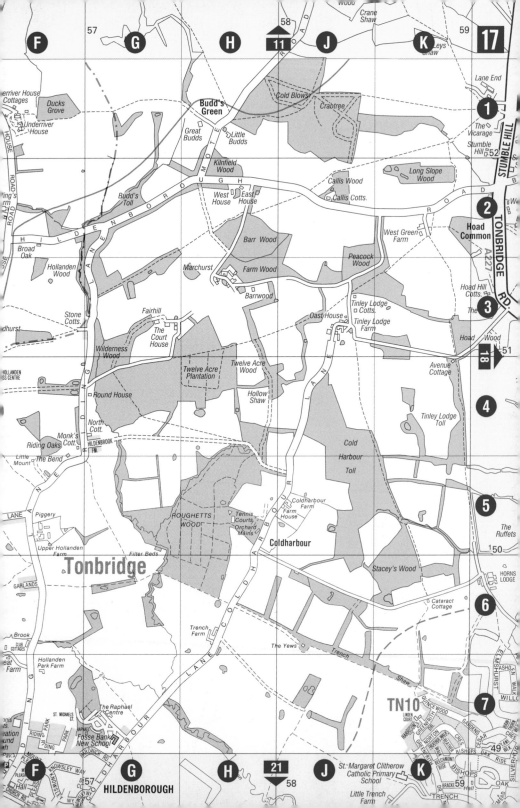

A map page showing the area around Leigh and Hildenborough.

Grid references and labels (top): 54 · **A** · **B** · 555 · **16** · **C** · **D** · 56 · **E** · B245

Place names and features:

49 · Bramber · Durham Farm · EGGPIE LANE · Home Farm · BOUNZELS · BUNZELS LANE · WATTS CROSS ROAD · Noble Tree Cross · B245 · Flat Wood · Church Hall · FOXBUSH · Hill · War Mem. · TONBRIDGE ROAD

The Haysel · The Cottage · Philpotts · Oakbourne · Mardens Wood · NOBLE TREE ROAD · The Lodge · Tennis Cts.

1 · Oldhouse Farm · Brook Cottage · Tips Cross · Wild Acre · Philpotts · RINGS HILL · Mountains · Sackville School

PHLOWER LANE · Greenacres · The Bungalow · Lower Street Farm · Reams Farm · Lucy's Farm · Ringshill Wood · **Hildenborough** · HILDEN GOLF COURSE · Stocks Green Wood · Club Ho.

2 · 148 · LOWER STREET · Hilden Health and Fitness Club · STOCKS GREEN · Bridge Cottage · GREEN

Summerthorn Wood · Chapel Cottage · Stocks Green Farm · **Stocks Green**

3 · The Kennels · Home Covert · Ashph Population · Weir · Bid Bridge · The Shoulder of Mutton · The Roundels · Meopham Bank

4 · 47 · Price's Farm · Hall Place Lake · Weir · Weir · Home Fm. · HOME FM · B2027 · The Alders · Kennards Farm · Barnett's Wood Picnic Site · Brook Cottages

5 · Price's Wood · Boat House · Hall Place · Park House · Moat Farm · Little Barnetts Farm · Ramh Mar

LEIGH · FORGE SQ. · War Mem. · The Green · THE FORSTAL · GARDEN COTTS · LINDON TREES JR · A21 · TONBRIDGE BY-PASS

6 · PENSHURST LODGE · B2027 · PENSHURST RD. HIGH STREET · DONKEY OAK · THE BUNGALOWS · FIELD COTTS · SAXBY COTTS · FLEUR DE LIS COTTS. · THE SQ · Sch · THE GREEN · GREEN VIEW AV. · LEALANDS AV. · Play. Fld. · Hollowtrees · Perrywinkle Shaw · MILL LANE · POWDER MILL LANE

PENSHURST RD. · Paul's Farm · Leigh · Sewage Works · CHARLOTTE COTTS · CHURCH HILL · CRANDALLS · MEADOW BANK · CLOSE · WINDHAM · WYNDHAM

46 · Rookery Wood · Old Park Ho. · Paul's Hill · ENSFIELD ROAD · RIVER MEDWAY · Weir · Mile Straight · Haysden Lake · FLOOD BARRIER · P

7 · MARTIN'S OK · Rough Ten Acres · Alder Cottages · River Medway · Slu Ga

Marl Pit · 54 · Ensfield Bridge · 555 · 555 · 56

Bottom labels: **A** · **B** · **C** · **26** · **D** · **E**

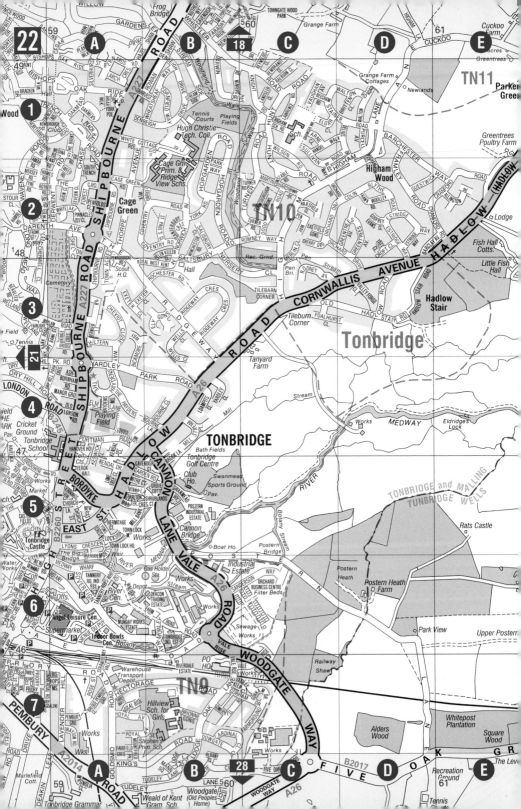

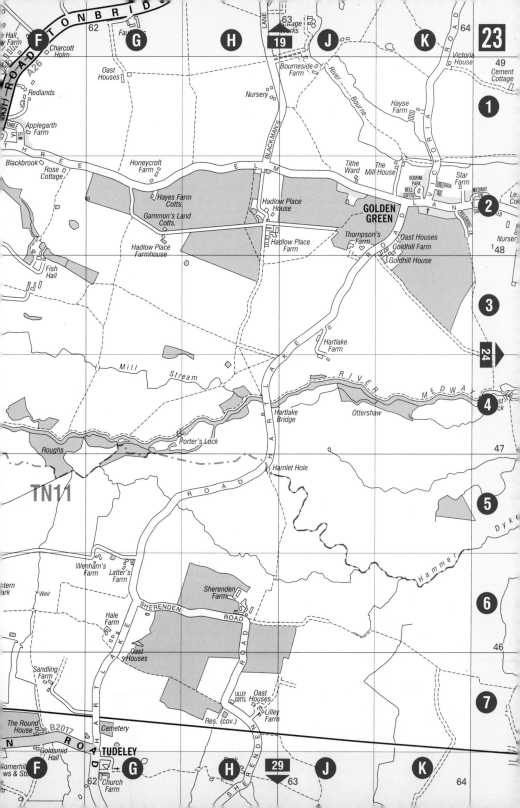

FTONBRIDGE
A26 EAST ROAD

Charcott Holm
Hall Farm
Faw...

Oast Houses

Redlands

Applegarth Farm

THREE Blackbrook

Rose Cottage

Honeycroft Farm

Nursery

Hayes Farm Cotts.

Gammon's Land Cotts.

Hadlow Place Farmhouse

Hadlow Place House

Hadlow Place Farm

BLACKMAN'S

Bourneside Farm

Nursery

River Bourne

Hayse Farm

Victoria House

49 Cement Cottage

1

Tithe Ward

The Mill House

BOURNE PARK
BELL COTTS.

VICTORIA

Star Farm

MEDWAY

GOLDEN GREEN

Thompson's Farm

Oast Houses
Goldhill Farm

Goldhill House

VECHES ROAD

Nurser

1 48

2

Fish Hall

Mill Stream

HARTLAKE

Hartlake Farm

RIVER

MEDWAY

3

24 ▶

Ottershaw

st Ck

4

Roughs

Porter's Lock

Hamlet Hole

Hartlake Bridge

47

Dyke

5

TN11

Hammer

ROAD

Wenham's Farm

Latter's Farm

ROAD

Weir

stern ark

Sherenden Farm

SHERENDEN

ROAD

6

Hale Farm

Oast Houses

46

Sandling Farm

HARTLAKE

Lilley Cotts.

Oast Houses

Lilley Farm

Res. (cov.)

SHERENDEN ROAD

7

The Round House

B2017

Cemetery

Goldsmid Hall

Somerhill ws & Sta

TUDELEY

Church Farm

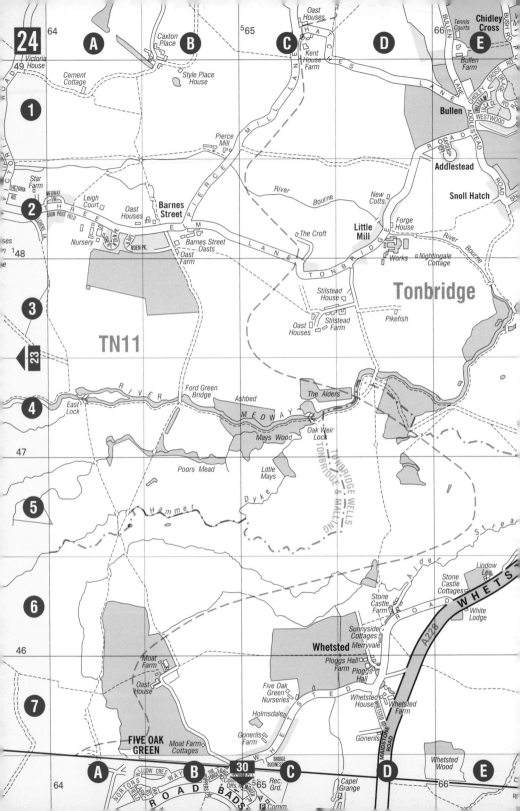

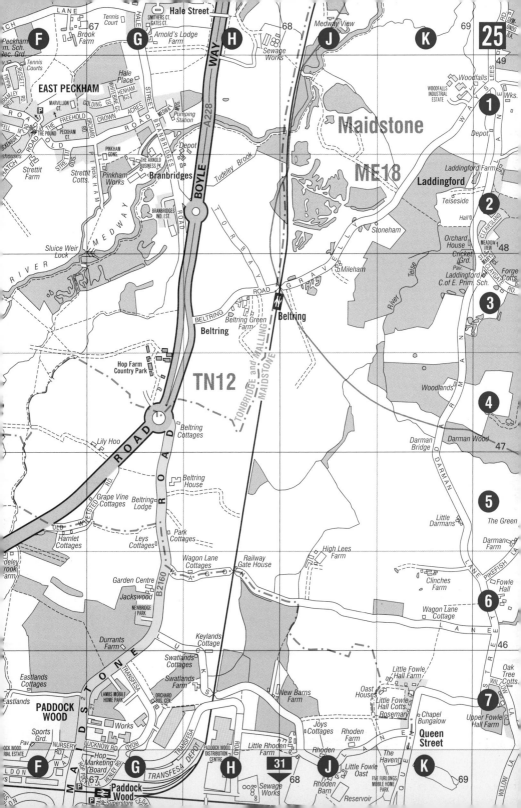

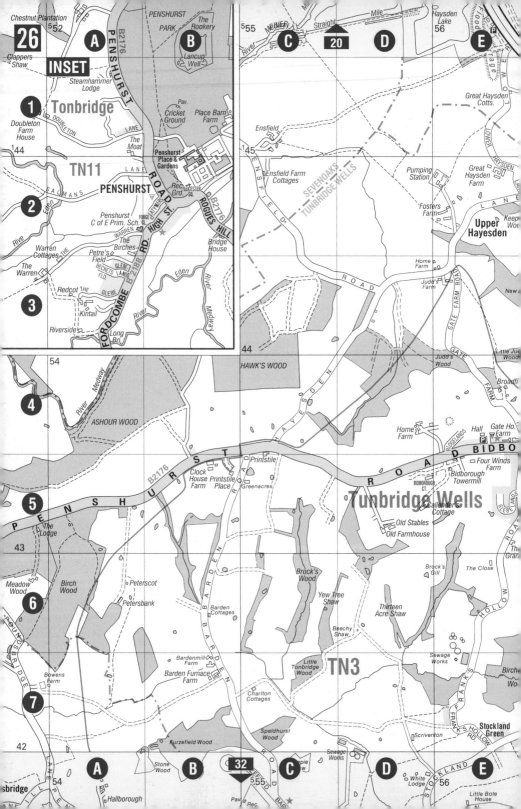

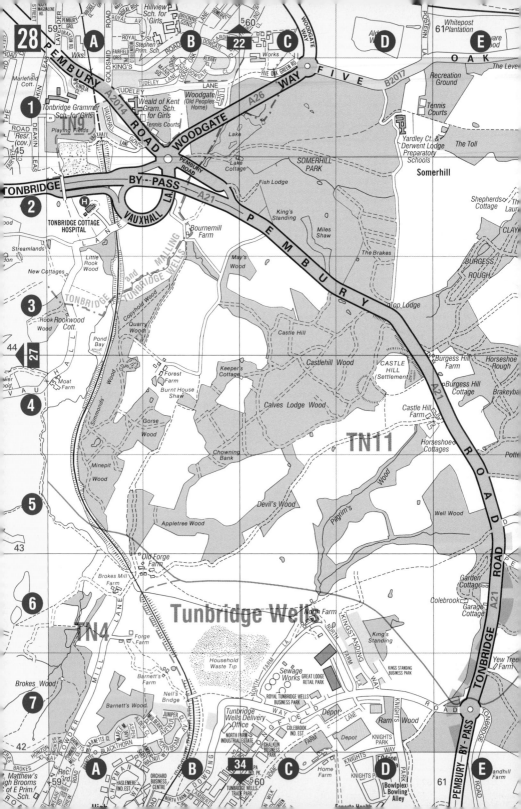

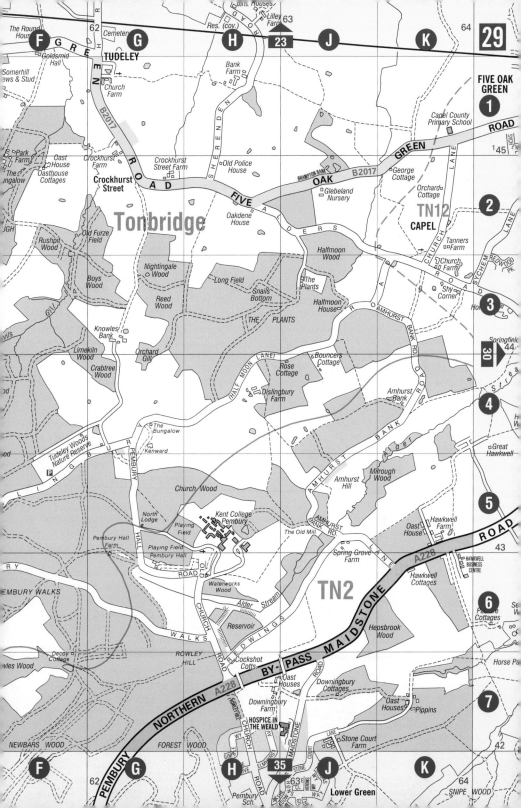

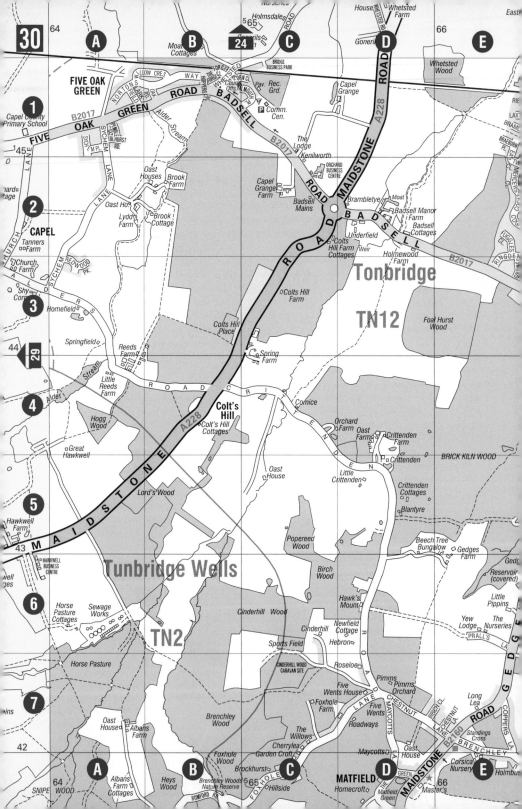

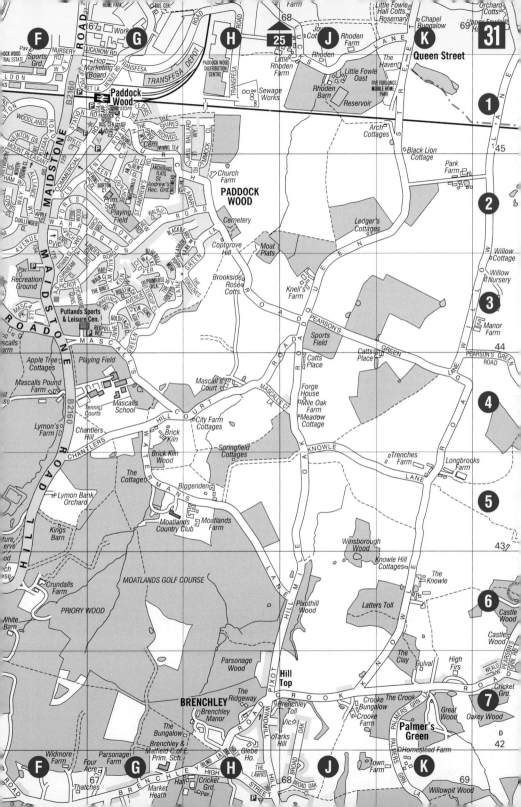

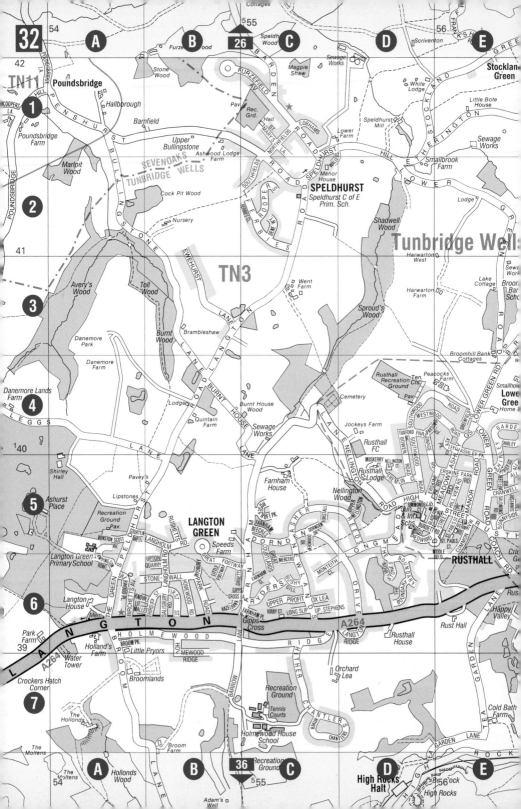

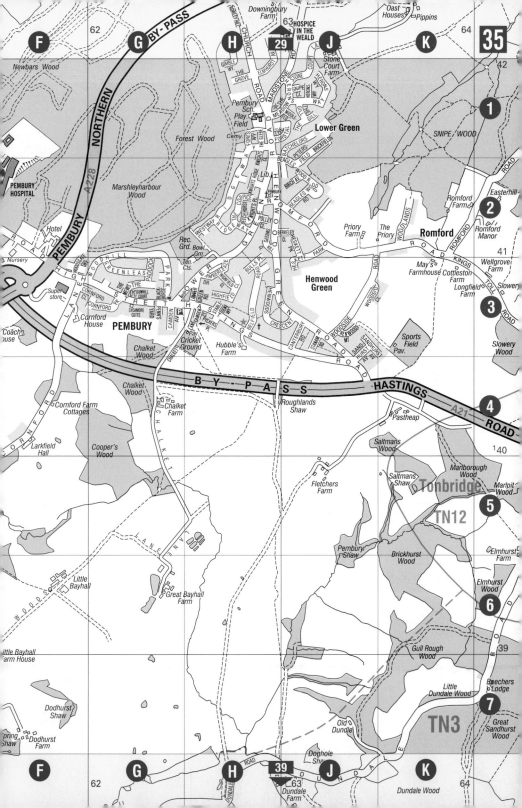

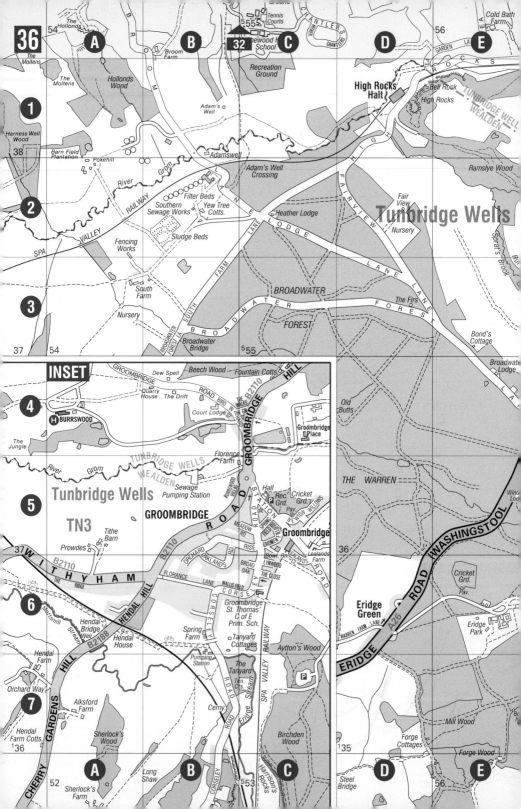

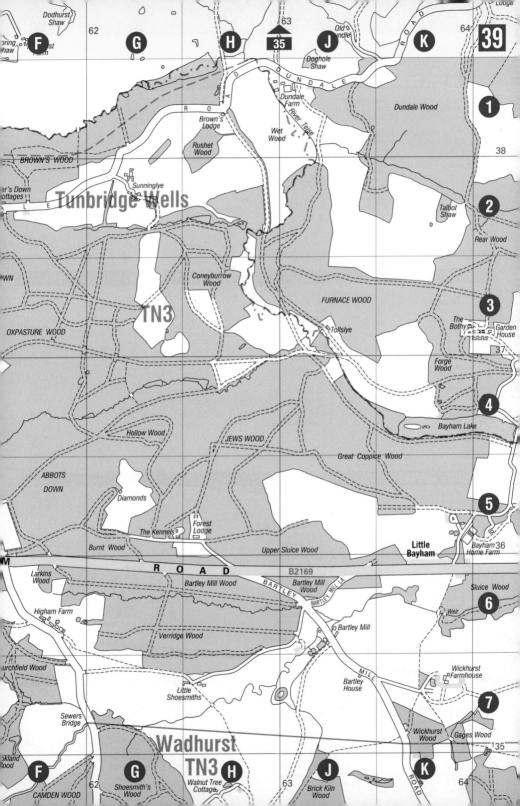

F · G · H · J · K

1
2
3
4
5
6
7

Dodhurst Shaw

Old Dundle

Doghole Shaw

Dundale Farm

Brown's Lodge

Rushet Wood

Wet Wood

River Teise

Dundale Wood

BROWN'S WOOD

Sunninglye

Tunbridge Wells

Talbot Shaw

Rear Wood

Coneyburrow Wood

FURNACE WOOD

The Bothy

Garden House

TN3

OXPASTURE WOOD

Tollslye

Forge Wood

Bayham Lake

Hollow Wood

JEWS WOOD

Great Coppice Wood

ABBOTS

DOWN

Diamonds

The Kennels

Forest Lodge

Burnt Wood

Upper Sluice Wood

Little Bayham

Bayham Home Farm

Larkins Wood

Higham Farm

R O A D

B2169

Bartley Mill Wood

Bartley Mill Wood

Sluice Wood

Weir

Verridge Wood

Bartley Mill

urchfield Wood

Bartley House

Wickhurst Farmhouse

Little Shoesmiths

Walnut Tree Cottage

Bartley House

Sewers Bridge

Wadhurst

TN3

Brick Kiln Wood

Wickhurst Wood

Gages Wood

CAMDEN WOOD

Shoesmith's Wood

F · G · H · J · K

INDEX

Including Streets, Places & Areas, Hospitals & Hospices, Industrial Estates,
Selected Flats & Walkways, Stations and Selected Places of Interest.

HOW TO USE THIS INDEX

1. Each street name is followed by its Postcode District and then by its Locality abbreviation(s) and then by its map reference;
e.g. **Addlestead Rd.** TN12: E Peck . . . .1E **24** is in the TN12 Postcode District and the East Peckham Locality and is to be found in square 1E on page **24**.
The page number is shown in bold type.

2. A strict alphabetical order is followed in which Av., Rd., St., etc. (though abbreviated) are read in full and as part of the street name;
e.g. **Ash Cl.** appears after **Ashburnham Rd.** but before **Ashcroft Rd.**

3. Streets and a selection of flats and walkways too small to be shown on the maps, appear in the index with the thoroughfare to which it is
connected shown in brackets; e.g. **Albion Row** *TN1: Tun W* . . . .4A **34** (off Albion Rd.)

4. Addresses that are in more than one part are referred to as not continuous.

5. Places and areas are shown in the index in **BLUE TYPE** and the map reference is to the actual map square in which the town centre or area is
located and not to the place name shown on the map; e.g. **BIDBOROUGH** 4E **26**

6. An example of a selected place of interest is Bough Beech Nature Reserve 7A **14**

7. An example of a station is **Bat & Ball Station (Rail)** 6J **3**

8. An example of a hospital or hospice is BURRSWOOD 4A **36**

GENERAL ABBREVIATIONS

All. : Alley	**Est.** : Estate	**Pde.** : Parade
App. : Approach	**Fld.** : Field	**Pk.** : Park
Arc. : Arcade	**Gdn.** : Garden	**Pas.** : Passage
Av. : Avenue	**Gdns.** : Gardens	**Pl.** : Place
Bri. : Bridge	**Ga.** : Gate	**Ri.** : Rise
Bus. : Business	**Gt.** : Great	**Rd.** : Road
Cvn. : Caravan	**Grn.** : Green	**Sq.** : Square
Cen. : Centre	**Gro.** : Grove	**Sta.** : Station
Chu. : Church	**Ho.** : House	**St.** : Street
Cl. : Close	**Ind.** : Industrial	**Ter.** : Terrace
Comn. : Common	**Info.** : Information	**Trad.** : Trading
Cnr. : Corner	**La.** : Lane	**Up.** : Upper
Cott. : Cottage	**Lit.** : Little	**Va.** : Vale
Cotts. : Cottages	**Lwr.** : Lower	**Vw.** : View
Ct. : Court	**Mnr.** : Manor	**Vs.** : Villas
Cres. : Crescent	**Mdw.** : Meadow	**Vis.** : Visitors
Cft. : Croft	**Mdws.** : Meadows	**Wlk.** : Walk
Dpt. : Depot	**M.** : Mews	**W.** : West
Dr. : Drive	**Mt.** : Mount	**Yd.** : Yard
E. : East	**Mus.** : Museum	
Ent. : Enterprise	**Nth.** : North	

LOCALITY ABBREVIATIONS

Addtn : **Addington**	Ide H : **Ide Hill**	Seal : **Seal**
A'hst : **Ashurst**	Igh : **Ightham**	S'oaks : **Sevenoaks**
Bell G : **Bell's Yew Green**	Ivy H : **Ivy Hatch**	S'brne : **Shipbourne**
Bidb : **Bidborough**	Kems'g : **Kemsing**	S'ham : **Shoreham**
Bor G : **Borough Green**	Knat : **Knatts Valley**	S'bgh : **Southborough**
Bras : **Brasted**	Ladd : **Laddingford**	Speld : **Speldhurst**
Brenc : **Brenchley**	Lamb : **Lamberhurst**	Sund : **Sundridge**
Chid : **Chiddingstone**	Lang G : **Langton Green**	Tonb : **Tonbridge**
Cous W : **Cousley Wood**	Leigh : **Leigh**	Tros : **Trottiscliffe**
Dun G : **Dunton Green**	Lye G : **Lye Green**	Tude : **Tudeley**
E Peck : **East Peckham**	Mark C : **Mark Cross**	Tun W : **Tunbridge Wells**
Eri G : **Eridge Green**	Mat : **Matfield**	Under : **Underriver**
Five G : **Five Oak Green**	Off : **Offham**	Wadh : **Wadhurst**
Ford : **Fordcombe**	Otf : **Otford**	Weald : **Weald**
Frant : **Frant**	Pad W : **Paddock Wood**	W King : **West Kingsdown**
Gold G : **Golden Green**	Pem : **Pembury**	W Mal : **West Malling**
Groom : **Groombridge**	Pens : **Penshurst**	W Peck : **West Peckham**
Hdlw : **Hadlow**	Plax : **Plaxtol**	Withy : **Withyham**
Hals : **Halstead**	Riv : **Riverhead**	Wro : **Wrotham**
Hild : **Hildenborough**	Rough : **Roughway**	Yald : **Yalding**
Horsm : **Horsmonden**	R'hall : **Rusthall**	

A

Abbey Ct. TN4: Tun W 4J **33**
Abbott Rd. TN15: Bor G 5D **6**
Acer Av. TN2: Tun W 2A **38**
Acorn Cl. TN12: Five G 1B **30**
Acorns, The TN13: S'oaks 1G **9**
ADDLESTEAD 2E **24**

Addlestead Rd. TN12: E Peck 1E **24**
Aisher Way TN13: Riv 6E **2**
Akehurst La. TN13: S'oaks 3J **9**
Albany Cl. TN9: Tonb 1B **28**
Albany Hill TN2: Tun W 4A **34**
Albert Cotts. TN1: Tun W 5A **34**
Albert Rd. TN9: Tonb 6K **21**
Albert St. TN1: Tun W 5K **33**
Albion Cl. TN11: Hdlw 6K **19**

Albion Rd. TN1: Tun W 4K **33**
Albion Row *TN1: Tun W* 4A **34**
(off Albion Rd.)
Alder Cl. TN4: S'bgh 7A **28**
Alders Mdw. TN9: Tonb 5H **21**
Alders Rd. TN11: Tude 2H **29**
TN12: Five G 2H **29**
Aldwych Cl. TN10: Tonb 7B **18**
Alexandra Rd. TN9: Tonb 7K **21**

Allan Cl. TN4: R'hall 5E 32
Allandale Rd. TN2: Tun W 3B 34
Allens La. TN15: Plax 6E 12
Alliance Way TN12: Pad W 2F 31
Allington Dr. TN10: Tonb 2E 22
Allington Rd. TN12: Pad W 1F 31
Allotment La. TN13: S'oaks 7J 3
All Saints Ri. TN4: Tun W 3J 33
All Saints Rd. TN4: Tun W 3J 33
Alma Pl. TN11: Hdlw 6J 19
Amberleaze Dr. TN2: Pem 3H 35
Amberley Cl. TN9: Tonb 7J 21
Amberley Ct. TN4: Tun W 1A 34
Amherst Hill TN13: Riv 1F 9
Amherst Rd. TN4: Tun W 4J 33
TN13: S'oaks 7H 3
Amhurst Bank Rd. TN2: Pem 5J 29
TN11: Five G 3K 29
Anchorage Flats TN12: Pad W 2G 31
Andrew Rd. TN4: Tun W 1A 34
Andrews Cl. TN2: Tun W 4B 34
Angel Indoor Bowls Cen. 6A 22
Angel La. TN9: Tonb 6K 21
Angel Leisure Cen. 6A 22
Angel Wlk. TN9: Tonb 6K 21
Annetts Hall TN15: Bor G 4E 6
Anthony Cl. TN13: Dun G 6E 2
Apple Barn Ct. TN15: Bor G 7G 7
Apple Ct. TN12: Pad W 2F 31
Appletons TN11: Hdlw 6J 19
Apple Tree La. TN2: Tun W 1B 34
(not continuous)
Argyle Rd. TN4: S'bgh 6J 27
TN13: S'oaks 3H 9
Armstrong Cl. TN14: Hals 1B 2
Arne Cl. TN10: Tonb 1C 22
Arnold Bus. Pk., The TN12: E Peck 2G 25
Arundel Cl. TN9: Tonb 7J 21
Arundel Rd. TN1: Tun W 7K 33
Ascot Cl. TN15: Bor G 5F 7
Ashburnham Cl. TN13: S'oaks 5J 9
Ashburnham Rd. TN10: Tonb 4A 22
Ash Cl. TN2: Tun W 2B 38
Ashcroft Rd. TN12: Pad W 3F 31
Ashden Wlk. TN10: Tonb 7A 18
Ashdown Cl. TN4: Tun W 5H 33
Ashenden Wlk. TN2: Tun W 1C 34
Asher Reeds TN3: Lang G 5C 32
Ashes La. TN11: Hdlw 5D 18
Ashgrove Rd. TN13: S'oaks 5G 9
Ashley Cl. TN13: S'oaks 2H 9
Ashley Gdns. TN4: R'hall 5E 32
Ashley Pk. TN4: R'hall 4E 32
Ashley Pk. Cl. TN4: R'hall 4E 32
Ashley Rd. TN11: Hild 2G 21
TN13: S'oaks 2H 9
Ash Platt Rd. TN15: Seal 6A 4
(not continuous)
Ash Platt, The TN15: Seal 5A 4
Aspen Way TN4: S'bgh 7A 28
Aspley St. TN4: R'hall 5F 33
Assembly Hall Theatre, The 5K 33
Athill Ct. TN13: S'oaks 7J 3
Auckland Rd. TN1: Tun W 3A 34
Audley Av. TN9: Tonb 5H 21
Audley Ri. TN9: Tonb 6H 21
Audrey Sturley Ct. TN4: R'hall 4F 33
Aultmore Ct. TN2: Tun W 6A 34
Avebury Av. TN9: Tonb 6K 21
Avenue Du Puy TN9: Tonb 6A 22
Avenue Rd. TN13: S'oaks 2J 9
Avenue, The TN9: Tonb 5K 21
TN15: Bor G 4E 6
Avon Cl. TN10: Tonb 2A 22
Avon St. TN1: Tun W 4A 34

B

Back La. TN11: S'brne 2A 18
TN13: Riv 7B 8
TN14: Ide H 7B 8
TN15: Igh 2A 12
TN15: S'oaks 2C 10
Baden Powell Rd. TN13: Riv 6E 2
Badgers Holt TN2: Tun W 4C 34
Badsell Rd. TN12: Five G, Pad W 1B 30
Baldwins La. TN4: Tun W 1A 34
Ballard Way TN12: Pad W 1H 31
Baltic Rd. TN9: Tonb 1J 27
Bancroft Rd. TN15: Wro 1D 6
Bank La. TN11: Hild 4C 16
TN15: Under 4C 16
Bankside TN13: Dun G 6D 2
Bank St. TN9: Tonb 5K 21
TN13: S'oaks 3H 9
Banner Farm Rd. TN2: Tun W 7K 33
Barchester Way TN10: Tonb 1D 22
Barclay Av. TN10: Tonb 2D 22
Barclay Fld. TN15: Kems'g 2A 4
BARDEN PARK 6H 21
Barden Pk. Rd. TN9: Tonb 6J 21
Barden Rd. TN3: Speld, Bidb 6B 26
TN9: Tonb 6J 21
BARNES STREET 2B 24
Barnetts Cl. TN4: S'bgh 7A 28
Barnetts Rd. TN11: Leigh 5C 20
Barnetts Way TN4: S'bgh 7A 28
Barnfield TN2: Tun W 3H 37
Barnfield Cres. TN15: Kems'g 2A 4
Barnfield Rd. TN13: Riv 1E 8
Barons Ct. TN4: Tun W 4J 33
Barretts Rd. TN13: Dun G 5D 2
Barrow La. TN3: Lang G 7B 32
Bartley Mill La. TN3: Lamb 6J 39
Bartley Mill Rd. TN3: Lamb, Wadh 6H 39
TN5: Wadh, Cous W 6H 39
BASTED 1D 12
Basted La. TN15: Bor G 1E 12
Basted Mill TN15: Bor G 6C 6
BAT & BALL 6J 3
Bat & Ball Ent. Cen. TN14: S'oaks 6J 3
Bat & Ball Rd. TN14: S'oaks 6J 3
Bat & Ball Station (Rail) 6J 3
Batchelors TN2: Pem 1J 35
Bates Hill TN15: Igh 7A 6
Battlefields Rd. TN15: Wro 1D 6
Bayhall Rd. TN2: Tun W 6A 34
Bayham Rd. TN2: Tun W 2J 37
TN3: Bell G 5D 38
TN3: Tun W 2J 37
TN13: S'oaks 1J 9
Bayley's Hill TN14: Weald, S'oaks 2E 14
Bayleys Hill Rd. TN8: Chid 7E 14
Beaconfields TN13: S'oaks 4F 9
Beacon Ri. TN13: S'oaks 4G 9
Beagles Wood Rd. TN2: Pem 2J 35
(not continuous)
Beatrice Wilson Flats TN13: S'oaks 3H 9
Beaulieu Rd. TN10: Tonb 3K 21
Becket Ct. *TN9: Tonb* *7K 21*
(off Alexandra Rd.)
Beckets Fld. TN11: Pens 3A 26
Bedford Rd. TN4: S'bgh 7J 27
Bedford Ter. TN1: Tun W 7J 33
Beecham Rd. TN10: Tonb 1C 22
Beeches, The TN2: Tun W 4B 34
Beech Hurst TN2: Pem 2H 35
Beechin Wood La. TN15: Bor G 7G 7
Beechmont Cotts. TN13: Weald 1H 15
Beechmont Ri. TN10: Tonb 1K 21
Beechmont Rd. TN13: S'oaks 7H 9
Beech Rd. TN13: S'oaks 3H 9
Beech St. TN1: Tun W 5K 33
Beechy Lees Rd. TN14: Otf 2K 3
Belfield Rd. TN2: Pem 3H 35
Belgrave Rd. TN1: Tun W 5K 33
Belgrove TN1: Tun W 7J 33
Bell Cotts. TN11: Gold G 2K 23
Bellows La. TN15: Bor G 5C 6
BELL'S YEW GREEN 5D 38
Bells Yew Grn. Rd. TN3: Frant, Bell G 6A 38
BELTRING 3H 25
Beltring Rd. TN4: Tun W 3J 33
TN12: Pad W 3H 25
Beltring Station (Rail) 3H 25
Benhall Mill Rd. TN2: Tun W 2A 38
TN3: Tun W 2C 38
Bentham Hill TN3: S'bgh 7F 27
Bentley's Mdw. TN15: Seal 5B 4
Berkeley Cl. TN2: Pem 2J 35
Berkeley Pl. TN1: Tun W 7J 33
Berkeley Rd. TN1: Tun W 7J 33
Berwick Way TN14: S'oaks 5H 3
BESSELS GREEN 2D 8
Bessels Grn. Rd. TN13: Riv 1D 8
Bessels Mdw. TN13: Riv 2D 8
Bessels Way TN13: Riv 2C 8
Betenson Av. TN13: S'oaks 7F 3
Bethel Rd. TN13: S'oaks 1J 9
Beulah Rd. TN1: Tun W 4K 33
Beverley Cres. TN9: Tonb 1H 27
Bewley La. TN15: Plax 3A 12
Bickley Rd. TN9: Tonb 7K 21
Bickmore Way TN9: Tonb 4A 22
BIDBOROUGH 4E 26
Bidborough Ct. TN3: Bidb 5D 26
Bidborough Ridge TN3: Bidb 4E 26
TN4: Bidb 4E 26
Bines, The TN12: Pad W 3G 31
Birch Cl. TN2: Tun W 2B 34
TN11: Hild 3F 21
TN12: Mat 7D 30
TN13: S'oaks 1H 9
Birches, The TN9: Tonb 1K 27
Birchetts Av. TN3: Lang G 6A 32
Birch Pl. TN13: S'oaks 2G 9
Birch Rd. TN12: Pad W 2G 31
Birch Way TN2: Tun W 2B 34
Birchwood Av. TN4: S'bgh 5G 27
Birchwood La. TN14: Dun G 1A 2
Birdcage Wlk. TN1: Tun W 6K 33
Bird in Hand St. TN3: Groom 4B 36
Birkdale TN1: Tun W 3K 33
Birken Rd. TN2: Tun W 3B 34
Birling Dr. TN2: Tun W 1J 37
Birling Pk. Av. TN2: Tun W 2K 37
Birling Rd. TN2: Tun W 2J 37
Bishop's Ct. TN4: Tun W 6G 33
Bishop's Down TN4: Tun W 6G 33
Bishop's Down Pk. Rd. TN4: Tun W 5G 33
Bishop's Down Rd. TN4: Tun W 6G 33
Bishops M. TN9: Tonb 7A 22
Bishops Oak Ride TN10: Tonb 7K 17
BITCHET GREEN 4F 11
Blackberry Way TN12: Pad W 2G 31
Blackhall La. TN15: S'oaks 1K 9
Blackhorse M. TN2: Pem 3G 35
Black Horse M. TN15: Bor G 6E 6
Blackhurst La. TN2: Pem 2E 34
TN2: Tun W 4C 34
Blackman's La. TN11: Hdlw 7H 19
Blackmead TN13: Riv 6E 2
Blacksole Cotts. TN15: Wro 1D 6
Blacksole La. TN15: Wro 1D 6
Blacksole Rd. TN15: Wro 1D 6
Blackthorn Av. TN4: S'bgh 7A 28
Blair Dr. TN13: S'oaks 1H 9
BLAKES GREEN 3F 11
Blakeway TN2: Tun W 2B 34
Blatchington Rd. TN2: Tun W 1J 37
Bligh's Mdw. *TN13: S'oaks* *3J 9*
(off High St.)
Bligh's Rd. TN13: S'oaks 3J 9
Blind La. TN12: Brenc 7H 31
Bliss Way TN10: Tonb 2C 22
Bluebell Walks TN12: Pad W 2G 31
Bogey La. TN4: Tun W 5H 33
Boleyn Rd. TN15: Kems'g 2A 4
Bondfield Cl. TN4: S'bgh 7J 27
Boneashe La. TN15: Bor G 6H 7
Bordyke TN9: Tonb 5A 22
BOROUGH GREEN 5D 6
Borough Green & Wrotham Station (Rail) 5D 6
Borough Grn. Rd. TN15: Igh, Bor G 6B 6
(not continuous)
TN15: Wro 2D 6
Bosville Av. TN13: S'oaks 1G 9
Bosville Dr. TN13: S'oaks 1G 9
Bosville Rd. TN13: S'oaks 1G 9
Botany TN9: Tonb 6A 22
Bottle Cotts. TN13: S'oaks 7G 3
Bough Beech Nature Reserve 7A 14
Bough Beech Reservoir Vis. Cen. 7A 14
Boundary Rd. TN2: Tun W 1B 38
Boundary, The TN3: Lang G 6D 32
Bounds Oak Way TN4: S'bgh 5G 27
Bourchier Cl. TN13: S'oaks 4H 9
Bourne Cl. TN9: Tonb 4B 22
Bourne Ind. Est. TN15: Bor G 4E 6
Bourne La. TN9: Tonb 4B 22
TN15: Plax 4D 12
Bourne Pk. TN11: Gold G 2K 23
Bourne Pl. TN11: Hild 7C 16
Bourne Pl. Mdws. TN11: Hild 7B 16
Bourne Va. TN15: Plax 5E 12
Bowen Rd. TN4: R'hall 4D 32
Bowlplex Bowling Alley
Tunbridge Wells 1D 34
Bowls Pl. TN12: Pad W 1G 31
BOWZELL GREEN 4F 15
Bowzell Rd. TN14: Weald 4F 15

Bowzells La. TN14: Weald, Chid 6E 14
Boyle Way TN12: E Peck 2H 25
Boyne Pk. TN4: Tun W 5H 33
Bracken Cl. TN2: Tun W 4C 34
Bracken Rd. TN2: Tun W 4C 34
Bracken Wlk. TN10: Tonb 1K 21
Bradbourne Ct. TN13: S'oaks 7H 3
Bradbourne Pk. Rd. TN13: S'oaks 1G 9
Bradbourne Rd. TN13: S'oaks 7H 3
Bradbourne Va. Rd. TN13: S'oaks 7F 3
Bradford St. TN9: Tonb 6K 21
Braeside Av. TN13: S'oaks 2F 9
Braeside Cl. TN13: S'oaks 1F 9
Bramble Cl. TN11: Hild 3G 21
Bramble La. TN13: S'oaks 6H 9
Bramble Wlk. TN2: Tun W 2B 34
Bramley Gdns. TN12: Pad W 1E 30
Bramley Rd. TN12: E Peck 1F 25
Brampton Bank TN11: Tude 2J 29
BRANBRIDGES 2G 25
Branbridges Ind. Est. TN12: E Peck 2G 25
Branbridges Rd. TN12: E Peck 1G 25
Brantingham Cl. TN9: Tonb 1H 27
Brattle Wood TN13: S'oaks 7H 9
Breedon Av. TN4: S'bgh 7H 27
BRENCHLEY 7H 31
Brenchley Rd. TN12: Mat, Brenc 7E 30
Brenchley Woods Nature Reserve 7B 30
Brendon Cl. TN2: Tun W 4B 34
Brent, The TN10: Tonb 1A 22
Bretland Rd. TN4: R'hall 5F 33
Brewery La. TN13: S'oaks 3H 9
Brian Cres. TN4: S'bgh 1K 33
Briar Wlk. TN10: Tonb 1A 22
Brickfields TN2: Pem 1J 35
Brickworks Cl. TN9: Tonb 2J 27
Brickworks Cotts. TN14: S'oaks 5K 3
Bridge Bus. Pk. TN12: Five G 1C 30
Bridge Cl. TN9: Tonb 7A 22
Bridge Ho. TN4: Tun W 4K 33
TN9: Tonb 5A 22
(off High St.)
Bright Ridge TN4: S'bgh 1G 33
Brindles Fld. TN9: Tonb 1J 27
Brionne Gdns. TN9: Tonb 7B 22
Brittains La. TN13: S'oaks 2F 9
Britten Cl. TN10: Tonb 1D 22
Broadcroft TN2: Tun W 2H 37
Broadgrove TN2: Tun W 1J 37
Broadhoath TN15: Ivy H 4G 11
Broadmead TN2: Tun W 2G 37
Broadmead Av. TN2: Tun W 2H 37
Broad Oak TN3: Groom 6C 36
TN12: Brenc 7J 31
Broad Oak Cl. TN2: Tun W 1H 37
TN12: Brenc 7J 31
Broadview Gardens 6H 19
Broad Wlk. TN15: S'oaks 6A 10
Broadwater Ct. TN2: Tun W 2G 37
BROADWATER DOWN 1H 37
Broadwater Down TN2: Tun W 2G 37
Broadwater Forest La.
TN3: Tun W, Groom 3B 36
Broadwater La. TN2: Tun W 1H 37
Broadwater Ri. TN2: Tun W 1H 37
Broadway, The *TN11: Hdlw 6J 19*
(off High St.)
Brockway TN15: Bor G 5E 6
Brokes Way TN4: S'bgh 1K 33
Brookfield TN15: Kems'g 2A 4
Brookfield Ct. TN4: S'bgh 7J 27
Brookfields TN11: Hdlw 6J 19
Brookhurst Gdns. TN4: S'bgh 5G 27
Brooklands TN2: Tun W 2B 34
Brook La. TN9: Tonb 5B 22
TN15: Plax 5E 12
Brookmead TN11: Hild 3F 21
Brook Rd. TN2: Tun W 2A 34
Brooks Cl. TN10: Tonb 7B 18
Brookside Cotts. TN2: Tun W 4D 34
BROOK STREET 1H 27
Brook St. TN9: Tonb 7H 21
Broomfield Rd. TN13: S'oaks 7F 3
BROOMHILL BANK 3F 33
Broomhill Pk. Rd. TN4: S'bgh 1G 33
Broomhill Rd. TN3: Tun W, S'bgh 3E 32
Broom La. TN3: Tun W, Lang G 6A 32
Broom Pk. TN3: Lang G 6A 32
Broughton Rd. TN14: Otf 1G 3
Brunger's Wlk. TN10: Tonb 2K 21
Brunswick Ter. TN1: Tun W 7J 33
Bubblestone Rd. TN14: Otf 1H 3
Buckhurst Av. TN13: S'oaks 3J 9
Buckhurst La. TN13: S'oaks 3J 9
Buckingham Rd. TN1: Tun W 7K 33
Bucklers Cl. TN2: Tun W 6A 34
BUDD'S GREEN 1H 17
BULLEN 1E 24
Bullen La. TN12: E Peck 1E 24
Bullfinch Cl. TN12: Pad W 3G 31
TN13: Riv 7D 2
Bullfinch Dene TN13: Riv 7D 2
Bullfinch La. TN13: Riv 7D 2
Bullingstone La. TN3: Speld, Pens 2A 32
Bullion Cl. TN12: Pad W 2F 31
Bull La. TN15: Wro 1E 6
Bulls Pl. TN2: Pem 3H 35
Bungalows, The TN11: Leigh 6A 20
Bunny La. TN3: Tun W 4F 37
Burdett Rd. TN4: R'hall 5D 32
Burns Cres. TN9: Tonb 1H 27
Burnt Ho. La. TN3: Lang G 4B 32
Burntwood Gro. TN13: S'oaks 5H 9
Burntwood Rd. TN13: S'oaks 6H 9
BURRSWOOD 4A 36
Burrswood Vs. TN3: Groom 5B 36
Burslem Rd. TN2: Tun W 3B 34
Burton Ct. TN12: Pad W 2G 31
Burwood Pk. TN2: Tun W 4C 34
Bush Rd. TN12: E Peck 1E 24
Bushy Gill TN3: Lang G 6C 32
Busty La. TN15: Igh 6B 6
Buttercup Cl. TN12: Pad W 3G 31
Butts, The TN14: Otf 1H 3
Byng Rd. TN4: Tun W 4G 33
Byrneside TN11: Hild 3G 21

C

Cabbage Stalk La. TN4: Tun W 7G 33
Cade La. TN13: S'oaks 6J 9
Cadogan Gdns. TN1: Tun W 5K 33
CAGE GREEN 2A 22
Cage Grn. Rd. TN10: Tonb 2A 22
Caister Rd. TN9: Tonb 6J 21
Caley Rd. TN2: Tun W 1B 34
Calverley Ct. TN1: Tun W 5K 33
Calverley Pk. TN1: Tun W 6K 33
Calverley Pk. Cres. TN1: Tun W 6K 33
Calverley Pk. Gdns. TN1: Tun W 5K 33
Calverley Rd. TN1: Tun W 5K 33
(not continuous)
Calverley Row TN1: Tun W 5K 33
Calverley St. TN1: Tun W 5K 33
Cambrian Rd. TN4: Tun W 2A 34
Cambridge Gdns. TN2: Tun W 7K 33
Cambridge St. TN2: Tun W 6A 34
Camden Av. TN2: Pem 3G 35
Camden Ct. TN1: Tun W 5K 33
TN2: Pem 3H 35
Camden Hill TN2: Tun W 6K 33
CAMDEN PARK 7A 34
Camden Pk. TN2: Tun W 7A 34
(not continuous)
Camden Rd. TN1: Tun W 5K 33
TN13: S'oaks 7H 3
Camden Ter. TN15: Seal 6B 4
Campbell Rd. TN4: Tun W 3J 33
Cannon La. TN9: Tonb 5B 22
Canterbury Cres. TN10: Tonb 2B 22
Canterbury Rd. TN2: Pem 3J 35
CAPEL 2K 29
Cardinal Cl. TN9: Tonb 7B 22
Carey's Fld. TN13: Dun G 5E 2
Carlton Cl. TN10: Tonb 7B 18
Carlton Cres. TN1: Tun W 5A 34
Carlton Pde. TN13: S'oaks 7J 3
Carlton Rd. TN1: Tun W 5A 34
Carpenters La. TN11: Hdlw 3G 19
Carrick Cl. TN10: Tonb 7C 18
Carrick Dr. TN13: S'oaks 1H 9
Carrs Cnr. TN1: Tun W 5K 33
CARTER'S HILL 6D 10
Carter's Hill TN15: Under 1D 16
Carville Av. TN4: S'bgh 7H 27
Castle Dr. TN15: Kems'g 2A 4
Castlefields TN9: Tonb 5K 21
Castle Rd. TN4: Tun W 7J 33
Castle St. TN1: Tun W 7J 33
TN4: S'bgh 6H 27
TN9: Tonb 5K 21
Castle Ter. TN11: Hdlw 6J 19
Castle Vw. TN11: Hdlw 6J 19
Catherine Pl. TN1: Tun W 5K 33
Cavalry Cl. TN10: Tonb 7C 18
Cavendish Av. TN13: S'oaks 7G 3
Cavendish Cl. TN10: Tonb 7B 18
Cavendish Ct. TN9: Tonb 5A 22
Cavendish Dr. TN2: Tun W 7K 33
Caxton La. TN11: Hdlw 6J 19
Caysers Cft. TN12: E Peck 1E 24
Cecil Burns Lodge TN2: Tun W 7B 34
Cedar Ct. TN4: Tun W 4J 33
Cedar Cres. TN10: Tonb 7A 18
Cedar Lodge TN4: Tun W 6H 33
Cedar Ridge TN2: Tun W 3B 34
Cedars, The TN12: Pad W 1G 31
Cedar Ter. Rd. TN13: S'oaks 1J 9
Cemetery La. TN11: Hdlw 5K 19
Chaffinch Way TN12: Pad W 3G 31
Chalket La. TN2: Pem 4G 35
Chalklin Bus. Pk. TN2: Tun W 7C 28
Challenger Cl. TN12: Pad W 2F 31
Chancellor Ho. TN4: Tun W 6H 33
Chancellor Way TN13: S'oaks 7G 3
Chandos Rd. TN1: Tun W 4A 34
Chantlers Hill TN12: Pad W 5F 31
Chapel Pl. TN1: Tun W 7J 33
Chapel Row TN15: Igh 6A 6
Chapel Vw. TN15: Igh 6A 6
Chapel Wlk. TN14: Ide H 1B 14
Chapman Way TN2: Tun W 1A 34
Charles St. TN4: S'bgh 1J 33
Charlotte Cotts. TN11: Leigh 5B 20
Charlton's Way TN4: Tun W 1G 37
Charlton Ter. TN9: Tonb 5A 22
Charne, The TN14: Otf 2G 3
Charterhouse Dr. TN13: S'oaks 1G 9
Chart Vw. TN15: Kems'g 2D 4
Chartway TN13: S'oaks 2J 9
Chase, The TN2: Tun W 7K 33
(not continuous)
TN10: Tonb 2A 22
TN15: Kems'g 1A 4
Chatham Hill Rd. TN14: S'oaks 6J 3
Chaucer Bus. Pk. TN15: Kems'g 3F 5
Chaucer Gdns. TN9: Tonb 1H 27
Chenies Cl. TN2: Tun W 2J 37
Cherry Gdns. Hill TN3: Groom 7A 36
Cherry Gro. TN10: Tonb 2C 22
Cherry Orchard, The TN11: Hdlw 5J 19
Cherry Tree Rd. TN2: Tun W 1G 37
TN10: Tonb 7B 18
Cherwell Cl. TN10: Tonb 2K 21
Chesfield Cl. TN11: Hdlw 6K 19
Chester Av. TN2: Tun W 7B 34
Chesterfield Dr. TN13: Riv 6D 2
Chestnut Av. TN4: S'bgh 1J 33
Chestnut Cl. TN4: S'bgh 1K 33
Chestnut La. TN12: Mat 7D 30
TN13: S'oaks 2H 9
Chestnut Wlk. TN9: Tonb 5H 21
(not continuous)
TN15: S'oaks 6B 10
CHEVENING 4A 2
Chevening Rd. TN13: Riv 6A 2
TN14: Sund 4A 2
Cheviot Cl. TN9: Tonb 3A 22
Chichester Dr. TN13: S'oaks 3F 9
Chichester Rd. TN9: Tonb 7J 21
CHIDLEY CROSS 1E 24
Chidley Cross Rd. TN12: E Peck 1E 24
Chieveley Dr. TN2: Tun W 1B 38
Childsbridge La. TN15: Seal, Kems'g 2B 4
Childsbridge Way TN15: Seal 5B 4
Childs Way TN15: Wro 1D 6
Chilston Cl. TN4: Tun W 4J 33
Chilston Rd. TN4: Tun W 4J 33
Chiltern Wlk. TN2: Tun W 5B 34
Chiltern Way TN9: Tonb 3A 22
CHIPSTEAD 7C 2
Chipstead La. TN13: Riv 7C 2
Chipstead Pk. TN13: Riv 7D 2
Chipstead Pk. Cl. TN13: Riv 7C 2
Chipstead Pl. Gdns. TN13: Riv 7C 2
Chipstead Sailing Club 7C 2
Chipstead Sq. TN13: Riv 7C 2
Christ Chu. Av. TN1: Tun W 6J 33
Church Fld. TN13: Riv 7F 3
Church Fld. Cotts. TN15: Seal 5B 4
Church Hill TN11: Leigh 5B 20
TN15: Plax 5C 12

Church La. TN3: Frant 6K **37**
TN9: Tonb 5A **22**
TN12: E Peck 1F **25**
Church Rd. TN12: Five G 3K **29**
TN15: Kems'g 2D **4**
TN1: Tun W 6H **33**
TN2: Pem 7H **29**
TN4: S'bgh 6H **27**
TN11: Hild 1F **21**
TN12: Pad W 1G **31**
TN14: Weald 3H **15**
TN15: Ivy H, Seal 1G **11**
TN15: Seal 6B **4**
Church St. TN9: Tonb 5A **22**
TN11: Hdlw 6J **19**
TN15: Seal 6C **4**
Church Vs. TN13: Riv 7E **2**
Cinderhill Wood Cvn. Site
TN12: Mat 7C **30**
Civic Way *TN1: Tun W* *6K* ***33***
(off Crescent Rd.)
Clanricarde Gdns. TN1: Tun W 6J **33**
Clanricarde Rd. TN1: Tun W 6J **33**
Clare Av. TN9: Tonb 6H **21**
Claremont Gdns. TN2: Tun W 7K **33**
Claremont Rd. TN1: Tun W 7K **33**
Clarence Rd. TN1: Tun W 6J **33**
Clarence Row TN1: Tun W 6J **33**
Clarendon Gdns. TN2: Tun W 1J **37**
Clarendon Pl. TN13: S'oaks 3G **9**
Clarendon Rd. TN13: S'oaks 2G **9**
Clarendon Way TN2: Tun W 1H **37**
Clare Way TN13: S'oaks 6J **9**
Clavadel Rd. TN12: Pad W 1G **31**
CLAYGATE **2D 18**
CLAYGATE CROSS **2E 12**
Claygate La. TN11: S'brne 1D **18**
Claygate Rd. ME18: Ladd 3K **25**
Clearway ME19: Addtn 3K **7**
Cleavesland ME18: Ladd 2K **25**
Cleeve Av. TN2: Tun W 7B **34**
Clenches Farm La. TN13: S'oaks 4G **9**
Clenches Farm Rd. TN13: S'oaks 4G **9**
Cleveland TN2: Tun W 5B **34**
Cleves Rd. TN15: Kems'g 2A **4**
Clifton Cotts. TN2: Tun W 1B **34**
Clifton Pl. TN1: Tun W 7K **33**
Clifton Rd. TN2: Tun W 2A **34**
Clockhouse TN2: Tun W 3D **34**
Clock Ho. La. TN13: S'oaks 1G **9**
(not continuous)
Close, The TN3: Groom 6C **36**
TN4: Tun W 1A **34**
TN13: S'oaks 2E **8**
TN15: Bor G 4E **6**
TN15: Igh 6B **6**
Clover Way TN12: Pad W 3G **31**
Club Cotts. TN11: Hild 6F **17**
Clyde Rd. TN10: Tonb 1A **22**
Coach & Horses Pas. *TN2: Tun W* *7J* ***33***
(off Market St.)
Coach Rd. TN4: R'hall 5E **32**
TN15: Ivy H, Igh 2J **11**
Cobbett's Ride TN2: Tun W 1H **37**
Cobbs Cl. TN12: Pad W 2F **31**
Cobden Rd. TN13: S'oaks 1J **9**
Cobhams TN3: Speld 1C **32**
Cobs Cl. TN15: Igh 6A **6**
Cogate Rd. TN12: Pad W 2E **30**
Cold Arbor Rd. TN13: Riv 2D **8**
COLDHARBOUR **5H 17**
Coldharbour La. TN11: Hild 1F **21**
Colebrook Ind. Est. TN2: Tun W 7C **28**
Colebrook Rd. TN4: Tun W 2A **34**
Coles Ct. TN2: Tun W 6A **34**
Colets Orchard TN14: Otf 1H **3**
Colin Blythe Rd. TN10: Tonb 2D **22**
College Av. TN9: Tonb 1H **27**
College Dr. TN2: Tun W 5B **34**
Collet Rd. TN15: Kems'g 2A **4**
Colne Rd. TN10: Tonb 2K **21**
Colonels Way TN4: S'bgh 6J **27**
COLT'S HILL **4B 30**
Commercial Rd. TN1: Tun W 4K **33**
TN9: Tonb 7K **21**
TN12: Pad W 2F **31**
Common Rd. TN11: Hdlw 4J **19**
TN15: Igh 7K **5**
COMMON, THE **3K 19**
Common Vw. TN4: R'hall 5E **32**
COMP **6J 7**
Comp La. ME19: Off 6K **7**
TN15: Bor G 6G **7**
Concord Cl. TN2: Tun W 5A **34**
TN12: Pad W 1E **30**
Coneyburrow Rd. TN2: Tun W 4C **34**
Coniston Av. TN4: Tun W 4G **33**
Connaught Way TN4: Tun W 4H **33**
Connections Ind. Cen.
TN14: S'oaks 4J **3**
Constable Rd. TN10: Tonb 2C **22**
Constant Mdw. TN13: S'oaks 3J **9**
Constitutional Hill Rd. TN4: S'bgh 7G **27**
Conyerd Rd. TN15: Bor G 5D **6**
Coombe Av. TN14: S'oaks 5H **3**
Coombe Ct. TN14: S'oaks 5H **3**
Coombe Rd. TN14: Otf 1J **3**
COOPER'S CORNER **6A 14**
Coopers La. TN11: Ford, Pens 1A **32**
Copper Beech Vw. TN9: Tonb 7J **21**
Copperfields TN2: Tun W 2K **37**
TN15: Kems'g 2B **4**
Copperfields Cl. TN15: Kems'g 2B **4**
Copperfields Orchard
TN15: Kems'g 2B **4**
Copperfields Wlk. TN15: Kems'g 2B **4**
Coppers Ct. TN4: S'bgh 1J **33**
Coppers La. TN12: Mat 7E **30**
Coppice, The TN2: Pem 2H **35**
Copse Bank TN15: Seal 5B **4**
Copse Rd. TN11: Hild 3G **21**
Copt Hall Rd. TN15: Igh 1J **11**
Corn Exchange *TN2: Tun W* *7J* ***33***
(off Pantiles, The)
Cornfield Way TN10: Tonb 1B **22**
Cornford Cl. TN2: Pem 3F **35**
Cornford La. TN2: Tun W, Pem 5C **34**
Cornford Pk. TN2: Pem 3G **35**
Cornwallis Av. TN10: Tonb 3C **22**
Correnden Rd. TN10: Tonb 3J **21**
Corseley Rd. TN3: Lye G, Groom 6B **36**
Cotman's Ash La. TN15: Kems'g 1F **5**
Cotman Way TN12: E Peck 1E **24**
Courtenwell TN3: Lang G 5A **32**
Courthope TN12: Pad W 2G **31**
Courtlands TN10: Tonb 3J **21**
Court La. TN11: Hdlw 6K **19**
Court La. Pl. TN11: Hdlw 6K **19**
(not continuous)
Court Mdw. TN15: Wro 1D **6**
Court Rd. TN4: Tun W 5G **33**
Court Royal TN4: Tun W 2G **37**
Courtwood Dr. TN13: S'oaks 2G **9**
Courtyard Gdns. TN15: Wro 1E **6**
Courtyard, The TN11: Hild 7C **16**
Coventry Rd. TN10: Tonb 2B **22**
Cramptons Rd. TN14: S'oaks 5H **3**
Crandalls TN11: Leigh 6B **20**
Cranford Rd. TN10: Tonb 2E **22**
Cranmer Rd. TN13: Riv 1E **8**
Cranwell Rd. TN4: R'hall 5E **32**
Crates Yd. TN4: Tun W 4J **33**
Crawshay Cl. TN13: S'oaks 1G **9**
Crendon Pk. TN4: S'bgh 7J **27**
Crescent Cotts. TN13: Dun G 5E **2**
Crescent Rd. TN1: Tun W 6K **33**
Crescent, The TN4: S'bgh 4G **27**
TN9: Tonb 5K **21**
TN13: S'oaks 6K **3**
TN15: Bor G 4E **6**
Cricketers Cl. TN3: Bell G 5E **38**
Crittenden Rd. TN12: Five G, Mat 4C **30**
CROCKHURST STREET **2G 29**
Croft Cl. TN10: Tonb 2D **22**
Croft Way TN13: S'oaks 3F **9**
Cromer St. TN9: Tonb 6J **21**
Cromwell Rd. TN2: Tun W 6A **34**
Crook Rd. TN12: Horsm, Brenc 7J **31**
CROSS KEYS **5G 9**
Cross Keys Cl. TN13: S'oaks 5G **9**
Crossway, The TN4: Tun W 7F **33**
CROUCH **1F 13**
Crouch La. TN15: Bor G 5E **6**
CROWDLEHAM **2F 5**
Crow Dr. TN14: Hals 1C **2**
Crow Hill TN15: Bor G 5E **6**
Crow Hill Rd. TN15: Bor G 5E **6**
Crowhurst La. TN15: Bor G 2B **12**
Crowhurst Rd. TN15: Bor G 6D **6**
Crown Acres TN12: E Peck 1G **25**
Crown Crest Ct. *TN14: S'oaks* *6J* ***3***
(off Seal Rd.)
Crownfields TN13: S'oaks 3H **9**
Crundwell Rd. TN4: S'bgh 7H **27**
Cuckoo La. TN11: Tonb 7D **18**
Culverden Av. TN4: Tun W 3H **33**
Culverden Down TN4: Tun W 4G **33**
Culverden Pk. TN4: Tun W 4H **33**
Culverden Pk. Rd. TN4: Tun W 4H **33**
Culverden Sq. TN4: Tun W 4J **33**
Culverden St. TN1: Tun W 5J **33**
Cumberland Ct. TN10: Tonb 3J **21**
TN13: Dun G 5E **2**
Cumberland Gdns. *TN1: Tun W* *7J* ***33***
(off Cumberland Yd.)
Cumberland M. *TN1: Tun W* *7J* ***33***
(off Cumberland Yd.)
Cumberland Wlk. TN1: Tun W 7J **33**
Cumberland Yd. TN1: Tun W 7J **33**
Cunningham Cl. TN4: Tun W 2K **33**
Cunningham Rd. TN4: Tun W 2K **33**
Currie Rd. TN4: Tun W 3J **33**
Cypress Gro. TN2: Tun W 2A **38**

D

Dale St. TN1: Tun W 5K **33**
Dane Rd. TN14: Otf 2E **2**
Danvers Rd. TN9: Tonb 6K **21**
Darent Cl. TN13: Riv 7C **2**
Darenth Av. TN10: Tonb 2K **21**
Darenth La. TN13: Dun G 6E **2**
Darman La. ME18: Ladd 4K **25**
TN12: Pad W 5K **25**
Darnets Fld. TN14: Otf 2F **3**
Darnley Dr. TN4: Bidb 4G **27**
Dartford Rd. TN13: S'oaks 2J **9**
Darwin Dr. TN10: Tonb 1B **22**
David Salomon's House 1F **33**
Davis Cl. TN13: S'oaks 7J **3**
Deacon Ct. TN4: Tun W 4J **33**
(Culverden Pk. Rd.)
TN4: Tun W 5H **33**
(Molyneux Pk. Rd.)
Deacon Trad. Est. TN9: Tonb 6B **22**
Deakin Leas TN9: Tonb 1K **27**
Deans Ct. TN9: Tonb 7K **21**
Decimus Pl. *TN1: Tun W* *5K* ***33***
(off Calverley Pk. Gdns.)
Delarue Cl. TN11: Tonb 5B **18**
Delius Dr. TN10: Tonb 1D **22**
Dell Dr. TN2: Tun W 5B **34**
Delves Av. TN2: Tun W 1A **38**
Denbeigh Dr. TN10: Tonb 1A **22**
Denbigh Rd. TN4: Tun W 2A **34**
Dene Lodge Cl. TN15: Bor G 5D **6**
Denesfield Ct. TN13: Riv 1B **8**
Dene, The TN13: S'oaks 4H **9**
Dene Way TN3: Speld 2C **32**
Dennington Ct. TN4: S'bgh 6J **27**
Derby Cl. TN11: Hild 1G **21**
Dernier Rd. TN10: Tonb 3A **22**
Derwent Dr. TN4: Tun W 4G **33**
Derwent Rd. TN10: Tonb 2A **22**
Devonshire Cl. TN2: Tun W 2G **37**
DIBDEN **5E 8**
Dibden La. TN14: Ide H, S'oaks 4E **8**
Dillon Way TN2: Tun W 3B **34**
Dimmock Cl. TN12: Pad W 2H **31**
Dippers Cl. TN15: Kems'g 2B **4**
Dislingbury Rd. TN11: Five G, Tude 5E **28**
Dodd Rd. TN10: Tonb 2C **22**
Donkey Fld. TN11: Leigh 6A **20**
Donnington Rd. TN13: Dun G 5D **2**
Doon Brae TN4: S'bgh 6J **27**
Doric Av. TN4: S'bgh 7H **27**
Doric Cl. TN4: S'bgh 7H **27**
Dorin Ho. TN1: Tun W 6A **34**
Dorking Rd. TN1: Tun W 3A **34**
Dornden Dr. TN3: Lang G 5C **32**
Dorset Rd. TN2: Tun W 7B **34**
Dorset St. TN13: S'oaks 3J **9**
Dorton Dr. TN15: Seal 7B **4**
(not continuous)
Doubleton La. TN11: Pens 1A **26**
Douglas Rd. TN9: Tonb 7J **21**
Dove Rd. TN10: Tonb 1K **21**
Dowding Way TN2: Tun W 1B **34**
Dower Ho. Cres. TN4: S'bgh 5G **27**
Dowgate Cl. TN9: Tonb 7B **22**
Downderry Nursery 1H **19**
Downs Ho. TN13: S'oaks 7J **3**

Downsview Rd. TN13: S'oaks 3F 9
Drage Rd. TN12: E Peck 1E 24
Draper St. TN4: S'bgh 6H 27
Dray Ct. TN11: Hdlw 6J 19
Drayton Rd. TN9: Tonb 7A 22
Driffield Gdns. TN9: Tonb 1H 27
Drive, The TN2: Tun W 1J 37
TN9: Tonb 1K 27
TN13: S'oaks 2H 9
Dry Bank Ct. TN10: Tonb 3A 22
Dry Bank Rd. TN10: Tonb 3K 21
DRYHILL 2B 8
Dryhill La. TN14: Sund 1B 8
Dry Hill Pk. Cres. TN10: Tonb 4A 22
Dry Hill Pk. Rd. TN10: Tonb 4K 21
Dry Hill Rd. TN9: Tonb 4K 21
Dryland Rd. TN15: Bor G 6D 6
Duchess' Wlk. TN15: S'oaks 3A 10
Dudley Keen Ct. TN9: Tonb 7B 22
Dudley Lodge TN2: Tun W 5A 34
Dudley Rd. TN1: Tun W 5J 33
Dukes Rd. TN1: Tun W 4A 34
Dunckley Vs. ME19: Addtn 3K 7
Dundale Rd. TN3: Tun W 2E 38
TN12: Mat 1J 39
DUNK'S GREEN 7E 12
Dunk's Grn. Rd. TN11: S'brne 1E 18
Dunorlan Farm Cotts. TN2: Tun W 5C 34
Dunorlan Pk. 6B 34
Dunstan Gro. TN4: Tun W 3K 33
Dunstan Rd. TN4: Tun W 3K 33
DUNTON GREEN 5E 2
Dunton Green Station (Rail) 4E 2
Durlings Orchard TN15: Igh 6B 6
Dux Hill TN15: Plax 5D 12
Dux La. TN15: Plax 4D 12
Dynes Rd. TN15: Kems'g 2K 3
Dynes, The TN15: Kems'g 2K 3
Dynevor Rd. TN4: Tun W 2A 34

E

Eaglestone Cl. TN15: Bor G 4E 6
Eardley Rd. TN13: S'oaks 2H 9
Earl's Rd. TN4: Tun W 5H 33
E. Cliff Rd. TN4: Tun W 3J 33
Eastfield Gdns. TN10: Tonb 2C 22
Eastlands Cl. TN4: Tun W 2G 37
Eastlands Rd. TN4: Tun W 2G 37
EAST PECKHAM 1F 25
East St. TN9: Tonb 5A 22
Eastwell Cl. TN12: Pad W 1E 30
Edenhurst TN13: S'oaks 3G 9
Eden Rd. TN1: Tun W 7J 33
Eden Wlk. TN1: Tun W 7J 33
Edgar Rd. TN15: Kems'g 2A 4
Edward St. TN4: R'hall 5D 32
TN4: S'bgh 7H 27
Egdean Wlk. TN13: S'oaks 1J 9
Eggpie La. TN11: Hild 5J 15
TN14: Hild 5J 15
Eldon Way TN12: Pad W 1F 31
Elgar Cl. TN10: Tonb 1C 22
Elizabeth Garlick Ct. *TN1: Tun W* *5K 33*
(off Goods Sta. Rd.)
Elmfield Cl. TN14: Weald 4H 15
Elm Gro. TN11: Hild 3H 21
Elmhurst Av. TN2: Pem 1H 35
Elm La. TN10: Tonb 4A 22
Elm Rd. TN4: S'bgh 7H 27
Elmshurst Gdns. TN10: Tonb 7A 18
Elmstead Cl. TN13: Riv 7E 2
Elphick's Pl. TN2: Tun W 2K 37
Ely Ct. TN1: Tun W 5K 33
Ely Gdns. TN10: Tonb 3B 22
ELY GRANGE 5A 38
Ely La. TN1: Tun W 5K 33
Emily Jackson Cl. TN13: S'oaks 2H 9
Ensfield Rd. TN11: Leigh 7A 20
Enterprise Ho. *TN9: Tonb* *6K 21*
(off Avebury Av.)
Ephraim Ct. TN4: Tun W 5H 33
ERIDGE GREEN 6D 36
Eridge Rd. TN3: Eri G 7D 36
TN4: Tun W 2G 37
Erskine Ho. TN13: S'oaks 3G 9
Erskine Pk. Rd. TN4: R'hall 5D 32
Esporta Health & Fitness Cen.
Tunbridge Wells 1D 34
Essex Cl. TN2: Tun W 2H 37
Estridge Way TN10: Tonb 2D 22
Etherington Hill
TN3: Tun W, S'bgh, Speld 2D 32
Evelyn Rd. TN14: Otf 1J 3
Ewehurst La. TN3: Speld 3B 32
Ewins Cl. TN12: Pad W 2G 31
Exedown Rd. TN15: Wro 1A 6
Exeter Cl. TN10: Tonb 3A 22

F

Fairfield Av. TN2: Tun W 4A 34
Fairfield Cl. TN15: Kems'g 3C 4
Fairfield Cres. TN9: Tonb 7A 22
Fairfield Rd. TN15: Bor G 4D 6
Fairfield Way TN11: Hild 2G 21
Fairlight Cl. TN4: S'bgh 6J 27
Fairlight Ct. TN10: Tonb 3K 21
Fairmile Rd. TN2: Tun W 4C 34
Fairview Cl. TN9: Tonb 2K 27
Fairview La. TN3: Tun W 2D 36
Fairways, The TN4: S'bgh 1J 33
Falmouth Pl. TN12: Five G 1C 30
Faraday Ride TN10: Tonb 7B 18
Farmcombe Cl. TN2: Tun W 7K 33
Farmcombe La. TN2: Tun W 7K 33
Farmcombe Rd. TN2: Tun W 7K 33
Farm Ct. TN4: Tun W 2G 37
Farmground Cl. TN9: Tonb 7C 22
Farm La. TN10: Tonb 3J 21
Farm Rd. TN14: S'oaks 5J 3
Farnaby Dr. TN13: S'oaks 4F 9
Farnham Beeches TN3: Lang G 5C 32
Farnham Cl. TN3: Lang G 6C 32
Farnham La. TN3: Lang G 6C 32
TN4: R'hall 6C 32
Farnham Pl. TN3: Lang G 6C 32
Farrance Ct. TN1: Tun W 5K 33
Farthingfield TN15: Wro 1E 6
FAWKE COMMON 5D 10
Fawke Comn. TN15: S'oaks, Under 4C 10
Fawke Wood Rd. TN15: Under 6C 10
Fell Mead TN12: E Peck 1F 25
Fellowes Way TN11: Hild 2G 21
Fen Mdw. TN15: Igh 3A 6
Fen Pond Cotts. TN15: Igh 3A 6
Fen Pond Rd. TN15: Igh 3A 6
TN15: Wro 1A 6
Ferbies TN3: Speld 2C 32
Ferbies Cl. TN3: Speld 2C 32
Ferdinand Ter. *TN3: Groom* *5C 36*
(off Corseley Rd.)
Ferholt TN10: Tonb 7A 18
FERNDALE 4A 34
Ferndale TN2: Tun W 5A 34
TN13: S'oaks 7J 3
Ferndale Cl. TN2: Tun W 5A 34
Ferndale Gdns. TN2: Tun W 5A 34
Ferndale Point TN2: Tun W 5A 34
Fernhurst Cres. TN4: S'bgh 6J 27
Fernside La. TN13: S'oaks 7K 9
Ferns, The TN1: Tun W 5A 34
TN15: Bor G 5G 7
Ferox Hall TN9: Tonb 5A 22
Ferringham TN4: Tun W 5H 33
Fiennes Way TN13: S'oaks 5J 9
FIG STREET 6G 9
Fig St. TN14: S'oaks 7F 9
Filmer La. TN14: S'oaks 6A 4
Filston La. TN13: Otf 1D 2
TN14: S'ham, Otf 1D 2
Firs Ct. TN4: Tun W 3H 33
First St. TN3: Lang G 6B 32
Fir Tree Cl. TN11: Hild 2G 21
Fir Tree Rd. TN4: Tun W 7H 33
Fishers Oak TN14: S'oaks 6J 3
Five Furlongs Mobile Home Pk.
TN12: Pad W 1J 31
FIVE OAK GREEN 1B 30
Five Oak Grn. Rd. TN11: Tonb, Tude 1C 28
TN12: Five G 2H 29
Flaxmore Pk. TN4: S'bgh 6J 27
Fleming Way TN10: Tonb 7C 18
FLETCHER'S GREEN 5J 15
Fleur De Lis Cotts. TN11: Leigh 6B 20
Floats, The TN13: Riv 6E 2
Florance La. TN3: Groom 6B 36
Flowerfield TN14: Otf 2F 3
Floyd Cl. TN4: Tun W 2J 33
Foalhurst Cl. TN10: Tonb 3C 22
Fordcombe Rd. TN11: Pens 3A 26
Ford La. ME19: Wro 3K 7
TN15: Wro 3K 7
Ford Pl. Cotts. TN15: Wro 2K 7
Forest Gro. TN10: Tonb 2A 22
Forest Rd. TN2: Tun W 2J 37
TN12: Pad W 2F 31
Forest Way TN2: Pem 1H 35
TN2: Tun W 1A 38
Forge Cl. TN11: Pens 2B 26
TN12: Five G 1B 30
Forge Cotts. TN14: Weald 4J 15
Forge La. ME18: W Peck 7K 13
Forge Rd. TN4: S'bgh 7H 27
Forge Sq. TN11: Leigh 5B 20
Forge, The TN12: Five G 1B 30
Forge Way TN12: Pad W 1G 31
Forstall TN3: Lang G 5C 32
Forstall, The TN11: Leigh 5C 20
Forstal, The TN2: Pem 1H 35
TN11: Hdlw 6K 19
Fort Rd. TN14: Hals 1C 2
Forum, The 7J 33
Fosse Bank Cl. TN9: Tonb 1J 27
Fosse Rd. TN9: Tonb 5K 21
Foxbury TN15: Bor G 5F 7
Foxbush TN11: Hild 1E 20
Foxgloves, The TN12: Pad W 3H 31
Foxhole La. TN12: Mat 7C 30
Fox Lea TN15: Bor G 5D 6
Framley Rd. TN10: Tonb 1D 22
Francis Rd. TN11: Hild 1F 21
Frankfield Ri. TN2: Tun W 1J 37
Frank's Hollow Rd. TN3: Tun W, Bidb 7E 26
Frank Woolley Rd. TN10: Tonb 2D 22
FRANT 7K 37
Frant Ct. TN3: Frant 7K 37
Frant Grn. Rd. TN3: Frant 6K 37
Frant Rd. TN2: Tun W 7J 33
TN3: Frant, Tun W 3J 37
Frant Station (Rail) 5D 38
Freehold, The TN11: Hdlw 5H 19
TN12: E Peck 1F 25
Fremlin Cl. TN4: R'hall 5D 32
Friars Way TN2: Tun W 3B 34
Friezeland Rd. TN4: Tun W 1F 37
Frog La. TN1: Tun W 7J 33
Frome Ct. TN10: Tonb 2K 21
Fuggles Cl. TN12: Pad W 2E 30
Fuller St. TN15: Seal 5D 4
Furnival Ct. TN2: Tun W 2H 37
Furzefield Av. TN3: Speld 1C 32

G

Gainsborough Gdns. TN10: Tonb 2C 22
Gallards Almshouses TN4: S'bgh 7J 27
Garden Cotts. TN11: Leigh 5C 20
Garden Ct. *TN13: S'oaks* *7K 3*
(off Garden Rd.)
Garden Rd. TN1: Tun W 5K 33
TN9: Tonb 5A 22
TN13: S'oaks 7K 3
Garden St. TN1: Tun W 5K 33
Garden Ter. TN15: Seal 6C 4
Gardyne M. TN9: Tonb 7K 21
Garlands TN11: Hild 6F 17
Garlinge Rd. TN4: S'bgh 7J 27
Garth Rd. TN13: S'oaks 6J 9
Garvock Dr. TN13: S'oaks 4G 9
Gasoline All. TN15: Wro 2H 7
Gate Farm Rd. TN3: Bidb 3E 26
Gate Ho. Wood Touring Pk. TN15: Wro 3J 7
Gates Ct. TN12: E Peck 1G 25
Gaza Trad. Est. TN11: Hild 7K 15
Gedge's Hill TN12: Mat 7E 30
Geographers' A-Z Map Company 4D 6
George St. TN2: Tun W 6A 34
TN9: Tonb 7K 21
Gibbetts TN3: Lang G 6B 32
Gilchrist Cotts. TN14: Weald 4J 15
Gill, The TN2: Pem 1J 35
Gimble Way TN2: Pem 1H 35
Gipps Cross La. TN3: Lang G 6B 32
Glade, The TN10: Tonb 7C 18
TN13: S'oaks 1H 9
Gladstone Rd. TN4: R'hall 5D 32
TN9: Tonb 6K 21
Glebe Ct. TN13: S'oaks 4H 9
Glebefield, The TN13: Riv 1F 9

Glebelands TN3: Bidb .5E **26**
TN11: Pens .3A **26**
Glebe La. TN13: S'oaks .5H **9**
Glebe Rd. TN14: Weald .3H **15**
Glebe, The TN2: Pem .1H **35**
TN3: Bidb .5E **26**
TN11: Pens .3A **26**
Glen Dunlop Ho., The TN13: S'oaks .7H **3**
Glenmore Pk. TN2: Tun W .2H **37**
Glyn Davies Cl. TN13: Dun G .5E **2**
GOATHURST COMMON .1B **14**
GODDEN GREEN .2C **10**
Godfrey Evans Cl. TN10: Tonb .2D **22**
GOLDEN GREEN .2K **23**
Goldfinch Cl. TN12: Pad W .3G **31**
Golding Gdns. TN12: E Peck .1G **25**
Golding Rd. TN13: S'oaks .7J **3**
Goldings TN12: Pad W .3E **30**
Goldsmid Rd. TN9: Tonb .1A **28**
Goods Sta. Rd. TN1: Tun W .5J **33**
Goodwins, The TN2: Tun W .1H **37**
Goodworth Rd. TN15: Wro .1D **6**
Gordon Rd. TN4: Tun W .2A **34**
TN13: S'oaks .3H **9**
Gorham Dr. TN9: Tonb .7B **22**
Gorse Rd. TN2: Tun W .4C **34**
GOVER HILL .7J **13**
Gover Hill ME18: W Peck .7J **13**
TN11: S'brne .1H **19**
Gover Vw. TN11: S'brne .6J **13**
Gracious La. TN13: S'oaks .1G **15**
Gracious La. End TN14: S'oaks .1F **15**
Grainger Wlk. TN10: Tonb .1C **22**
Grampian Cl. TN2: Tun W .4B **34**
Granary TN12: Pad W .2H **31**
Grange Gdns. TN4: R'hall .5F **33**
Grange Hill TN15: Plax .5C **12**
Grange Rd. TN4: R'hall .5F **33**
TN11: S'brne .1B **18**
TN13: S'oaks .5G **9**
TN15: Bor G .5G **7**
Granville Rd. TN1: Tun W .4A **34**
TN13: S'oaks .2G **9**
Grassy La. TN13: S'oaks .4H **9**
Gravelly Ways ME18: Ladd, Pad W .3J **25**
Gravesend Rd. TN15: Wro .1E **6**
Gt. Bounds Dr. TN4: S'bgh .5G **27**
Gt. Brooms Rd. TN4: Tun W .1K **33**
Great Comp Garden .6J **7**
Gt. Courtlands TN3: Lang G .5C **32**
Great Elms TN11: Hdlw .5J **19**
Gt. Footway TN3: Lang G .6B **32**
Gt. Hall Arc. TN1: Tun W .6K **33**
Gt. Hollanden Bus. Cen.
TN15: Under .4F **17**
Gt. Lodge Retail Pk. TN2: Tun W .7C **28**
GREATNESS .6J **3**
Greatness La. TN14: S'oaks .6J **3**
Greatness Rd. TN14: S'oaks .6J **3**
Gt. Till Cl. TN14: Otf .1E **2**
Grecian Rd. TN1: Tun W .7K **33**
Greenfield Cl. TN4: R'hall .4E **32**
Greenfrith Dr. TN10: Tonb .7K **17**
Greenlands TN15: Bor G .5F **7**
Greenlands Rd. TN15: Kems'g .4D **4**
Green La. TN12: Pad W .3G **31**
Green La., The TN11: Leigh .6B **20**
Greenleas TN2: Pem .3G **35**
Greensand Way ME18: W Peck .1J **19**
TN11: S'brne .1J **19**
Green, The TN3: Frant .7K **37**
TN3: Groom .4C **36**
TN3: Lang G .6A **32**
TN11: Leigh .6B **20**
TN12: Mat .7D **30**
TN13: S'oaks .7K **3**
TN14: Otf .1H **3**
TN15: Seal .6B 4
(off Church Rd.)
Greentrees Av. TN10: Tonb .2D **22**
Green Vw. Av. TN11: Leigh .6C **20**
Greenview Cres. TN11: Hild .3G **21**
Green Way TN2: Tun W .1C **34**
Greenways, The TN12: Pad W .3F **31**
Greenwood Pl. TN15: Wro .2E **6**
Greenwood Way TN13: S'oaks .3F **9**
Greggs Wood Rd. TN2: Tun W .2B **34**
Gresham Cl. TN10: Tonb .7C **18**
Greystones Cl. TN15: Kems'g .2A **4**
Griggs Way TN15: Bor G .5E **6**
Gromenfield TN3: Groom .5C **36**
GROOMBRIDGE .5C **36**
Groombridge Hill TN3: Groom .4C **36**
Groombridge Place .4C **36**
Groombridge Rd.
TN3: Ford, A'hst, Groom .4A **36**
Groombridge Station
Spa Valley Railway .5C **36**
Grosvenor Bri. TN1: Tun W .4K **33**
Grosvenor Pk. TN1: Tun W .5J **33**
Grosvenor Pl. TN1: Tun W .3K **33**
Grosvenor Rd. TN1: Tun W .5J **33**
Grosvenor Wlk. TN1: Tun W .5J **33**
Grove Av. TN1: Tun W .7J **33**
Grove Cott. TN9: Tonb .5B **22**
Grove Hill Gdns. TN1: Tun W .7K **33**
Grove Hill Rd. TN1: Tun W .6K **33**
Grove Rd. TN14: S'oaks .6J **3**
TN15: Seal .6C **4**
Grover St. TN1: Tun W .5K **33**
Grove, The TN2: Pem .1H **35**
Guestwick TN10: Tonb .2D **22**
Guildford Rd. TN1: Tun W .6K **33**

H

Hadley Ct. TN4: Tun W .3H **33**
HADLOW .6J **19**
Hadlow Pk. TN11: Hdlw .5J **19**
Hadlow Rd. TN9: Tonb .5A **22**
TN10: Tonb, Hdlw .2E **22**
TN11: Tonb, Hdlw .2E **22**
Hadlow Rd. E. TN10: Tonb .2E **22**
TN11: Tonb .2E **22**
HADLOW STAIR .3D **22**
Hadlow Stair Rd. TN10: Tonb .3D **22**
Hailstone Cl. TN11: Hdlw .6J **19**
Hale La. TN14: Otf .2F **3**
Hale Oak Rd. TN14: Weald .5G **15**
HALE STREET .1G **25**
Hale St. TN12: E Peck .1G **25**
Half Moon La. TN11: Hild .1F **21**
TN11: Tude .4H **29**
Hall Hill TN15: Seal .1D **10**
HALL'S GREEN .7G **15**
Hall's Hole Rd. TN2: Tun W .7B **34**
Hamble Rd. TN10: Tonb .2K **21**
Hamilton Ct. TN4: Tun W .4J **33**
Hamilton Ho. TN4: Tun W .4J **33**
Hamlin Rd. TN13: Riv .7E **2**
Hamlyn Ct. TN13: Dun G .6E **2**
Hamptons Rd.
TN11: S'brne, Hdlw .1D **18**
Handel Wlk. TN10: Tonb .1C **22**
HANGING BANK .3A **14**
Hanging Bank Nature Reserve .2B **14**
Hanover Ho. TN9: Tonb .4A **22**
Hanover Rd. TN1: Tun W .5J **33**
Hardinge Av. TN4: S'bgh .5G **27**
Hardwick Rd. TN11: Hild .7G **17**
Hardy's Yd. TN13: Dun G .6E **2**
Harescroft TN2: Tun W .2H **37**
Hargate Cl. TN2: Tun W .3H **37**
Harland Way TN4: S'bgh .4G **27**
Harmer Ct. TN4: S'bgh .6J **27**
Harmony St. TN4: R'hall .5F **33**
Harries Rd. TN2: Tun W .2B **34**
Harrison Rd. TN15: Bor G .5D **6**
Harrison's Rocks .7C **36**
Harrison Way TN13: S'oaks .7G **3**
Hartfield Cl. TN10: Tonb .2C **22**
Hartlake Rd. TN11: Five G, Gold G .4H **23**
TN11: Tude .7G **23**
Hartslands Rd. TN13: S'oaks .1J **9**
Harvest Rd. TN10: Tonb .1A **22**
Haslemere Ind. Est. TN2: Tun W .1A **34**
Hasletts Cl. TN1: Tun W .3K **33**
Hastings Rd. TN2: Pem .3H **35**
TN12: Mat .4K **35**
Hatches La. TN12: E Peck .1C **24**
Havelock Rd. TN9: Tonb .4K **21**
Havering Cl. TN2: Tun W .3D **34**
Hawden Cl. TN11: Hild .3H **21**
Hawden La. TN11: Hild .3H **21**
Hawden Rd. TN9: Tonb .5K **21**
HAWKENBURY .7B **34**
Hawkenbury Cl. TN2: Tun W .7B **34**
Hawkenbury Mead TN2: Tun W .1B **38**
Hawkenbury Rd. TN2: Tun W .1B **38**
TN3: Tun W .1B **38**
Hawkes Pl. TN13: S'oaks .5G **9**
Hawkwell Bus. Cen. TN2: Pem .6K **29**
Hawthorn La. TN13: S'oaks .7F **3**
Hawthorn Wlk. TN2: Tun W .1C **34**
TN10: Tonb .7A **18**
Haydens M. TN9: Tonb .4A **22**
Haydens, The TN9: Tonb .4A **22**
Hayesden La. TN11: Tonb .4C **26**
Haysden Country Pk. .7G **21**
Haywain Cl. TN12: Pad W .3G **31**
Hazelbank TN3: Lang G .6B **32**
Hazel Shaw TN10: Tonb .7A **18**
Hazelwood Cl. TN2: Tun W .1B **34**
Heather Bank TN12: Pad W .2G **31**
Heather Wlk. TN10: Tonb .7K **17**
(not continuous)
Heathfield Rd. TN13: S'oaks .7F **3**
Heathfields TN2: Tun W .5B **34**
HEAVERHAM .2G **5**
Heaverham Rd. TN15: Kems'g .2D **4**
Hectorage Rd. TN9: Tonb .7A **22**
Helen Keller Cl. TN10: Tonb .2B **22**
Hendal Hill TN3: Groom .6A **36**
Henham Gdns. TN12: E Peck .1G **25**
Henley Cl. TN2: Tun W .4A **34**
Henley Rd. TN12: Pad W .1G **31**
HENWOOD GREEN .3J **35**
Henwood Grn. Rd. TN2: Pem .2H **35**
Henwoods Cres. TN2: Pem .3H **35**
Henwoods Mt. TN2: Pem .3J **35**
Hermitage Ct. TN9: Tonb .5A **22**
Hern, The TN15: Bor G .7G **7**
Herons Way TN2: Pem .1J **35**
Hertsfield Ho. *TN9: Tonb .7K 21*
(off Quarry Hill Rd.)
Heskett Pk. TN2: Pem .2J **35**
Higham Gdns. TN10: Tonb .1D **22**
Higham La. TN10: Tonb .3C **22**
TN11: Tonb .5C **18**
Higham School Rd. TN10: Tonb .1C **22**
HIGHAM WOOD .2C **22**
High Beeches TN2: Tun W .3B **34**
HIGH BROOMS .2A **34**
High Brooms Rd. TN4: Tun W .1K **33**
High Brooms Station (Rail) .2A **34**
High Cross Rd. TN15: Ivy H .4K **11**
Highfield Cl. TN2: Pem .3H **35**
Highfield Rd. TN4: Tun W .2A **34**
TN15: Kems'g .1A **4**
Highgrove TN2: Tun W .2J **37**
High Hilden Cl. TN10: Tonb .3J **21**
High Ho. La. TN11: Hdlw .6F **19**
Highlands TN2: Tun W .2B **34**
Highlands Ho. TN1: Tun W .6A **34**
Highlands Pk. TN15: Seal .6A **4**
High Rocks .1D **36**
High Rocks Halt Station
Spa Valley Railway .1D **36**
High Rocks La. TN3: Tun W .1D **36**
High St. TN1: Tun W .7J **33**
TN2: Pem .3F **35**
TN3: Bidb .5E **26**
TN3: Frant .6A **38**
TN4: R'hall .5D **32**
TN9: Tonb .6K **21**
TN11: Hdlw .6J **19**
TN11: Leigh .6A **20**
TN11: Pens .2B **26**
TN12: Brenc .7H **31**
TN13: Riv .7C **2**
TN13: S'oaks .3J **9**
TN14: Otf .1G **3**
TN15: Bor G .5D **6**
TN15: Kems'g .2D **4**
TN15: Seal .6B **4**
TN15: Wro .1E **6**
High Woods La. TN2: Tun W, Pem .7B **34**
(not continuous)
Hilbert Cl. TN2: Tun W .4A **34**
Hilbert Rd. TN2: Tun W .3A **34**
Hilden Av. TN11: Hild .3H **21**
HILDENBOROUGH .2G **21**
Hildenborough Rd. TN11: Leigh .5B **20**
TN11: S'brne, Under .2F **17**
Hildenborough Station (Rail) .1D **20**
Hildenbrook Farm TN11: Hild .4G **17**
Hilden Health and Fitness Club .2D **20**
HILDEN PARK .2H **21**
Hilden Pk. Rd. TN11: Hild .3H **21**
Hillborough Av. TN13: S'oaks .7K **3**
Hill Crest TN13: S'oaks .7G **3**
Hillcrest TN4: S'bgh .1K **33**

Hillcrest Dr. TN2: Tun W . . . 2B 34
Hillfield Rd. TN13: Dun G . . . 5E 2
Hillgarth TN4: S'bgh . . . 1J 33
Hillingdon Av. TN13: S'oaks . . . 6J 3
Hillingdon Ri. TN13: S'oaks . . . 7K 3
Hillside TN9: Tonb . . . 1J 27
Hillside Rd. TN13: S'oaks . . . 1K 9
TN15: Kems'g . . . 2B 4
Hill St. TN1: Tun W . . . 4K 33
HILL TOP . . . 7J 31
Hilltop TN9: Tonb . . . 1K 27
Hill Vw. TN15: Bor G . . . 5E 6
Hillview TN15: Bor G . . . 1D 12
Hill Vw. Cl. TN15: Bor G . . . 5E 6
Hill Vw. Rd. TN4: R'hall . . . 5E 32
TN11: Hild . . . 2H 21
Hitchen Hatch La. TN13: S'oaks . . . 2G 9
Hither Chantlers TN3: Lang G . . . 7C 32
HOAD COMMON . . . 2A 18
Holden Cnr. TN4: S'bgh . . . 7G 27
Holden Pk. Rd. TN4: S'bgh . . . 1H 33
Holden Rd. TN4: S'bgh . . . 7G 27
Holford St. TN9: Tonb . . . 6K 21
Hollin Cl. TN4: Tun W . . . 5H 33
Hollow Trees Dr. TN11: Leigh . . . 5C 20
Holly Bank TN12: Brenc . . . 7H 31
Holly Bush Cl. TN13: S'oaks . . . 2J 9
Holly Bush Ct. TN13: S'oaks . . . 2J 9
Holly Bush La. TN13: S'oaks . . . 2J 9
Holly Bush Sports Complex . . . 2J 9
Hollyshaw Cl. TN2: Tun W . . . 7A 34
Holmesdale Rd. TN13: S'oaks . . . 1J 9
Holmewood Ridge TN3: Lang G . . . 6A 32
Holmewood Rd. TN4: Tun W . . . 2A 34
Holmhurst Cl. TN4: Tun W . . . 5H 33
Holyoake Ter. TN13: S'oaks . . . 2G 9
Homedean Rd. TN13: Riv . . . 7C 2
Home Farm Cl. TN11: Leigh . . . 4C 20
Home Farm Ct. TN3: Frant . . . 6A 38
Home Farm La. TN2: Tun W . . . 1C 34
Homefield Rd. TN13: Riv . . . 7E 2
Homewood Rd. TN3: Lang G . . . 6B 32
HOMOEOPATHIC HOSPITAL . . . 6J 33
Honeypot La. TN15: Kems'g . . . 4D 4
Hoopers Yd. TN13: S'oaks . . . 4J 9
Hope Av. TN11: Hdlw . . . 5H 19
Hop Farm Country Pk. . . . 4G 25
Hopgarden La. TN13: S'oaks . . . 6G 9
Hopgarden Rd. TN10: Tonb . . . 2B 22
Hoppers TN12: Five G . . . 1B 30
Hop Pocket La. TN12: Pad W . . . 1F 31
Hopwood Gdns. TN4: Tun W . . . 3J 33
Horizon Cl. TN4: S'bgh . . . 1K 33
Horlingham Cl. TN10: Tonb . . . 7B 18
Hornbeam Av. TN4: S'bgh . . . 7B 28
Hornbeam Cl. TN12: Pad W . . . 3F 31
Horns Lodge TN11: Tonb . . . 6A 18
HOSPICE IN THE WEALD . . . 7J 29
Hospital Rd. TN13: S'oaks . . . 6J 3
Houselands Rd. TN9: Tonb . . . 5K 21
Howard Gdns. TN2: Tun W . . . 1J 37
Howlands TN15: Wro . . . 1D 6
Hubbard's Hill TN13: Weald . . . 1H 15
TN14: Weald . . . 2H 15
Humboldt Ct. TN2: Tun W . . . 4B 34
HUNGERSHALL PARK . . . 7G 33
Hungershall Pk. TN4: Tun W . . . 7F 33
Hungershall Pk. Cl. TN4: Tun W . . . 7F 33
Hunsdon Dr. TN13: S'oaks . . . 1H 9
Hunter Seal TN11: Leigh . . . 5G 21
Hunters Health and Fitness Club . . . *6K 21*
(off Avebury Av.)
Hunters Way TN2: Tun W . . . 1H 37
Huntley Gdns. TN4: Tun W . . . 3G 33
Huntleys Pk. TN4: Tun W . . . 4H 33
Hunt Rd. TN10: Tonb . . . 1C 22
Hunts Farm Cl. TN15: Bor G . . . 5E 6
Huntsman La. TN15: Wro . . . 3J 7
Hurst Farm Rd. TN14: Weald . . . 3H 15
Hurst La. TN14: Weald . . . 4H 15
(not continuous)
Hurst, The ME18: S'brne, Bor G . . . 5H 13
TN2: Tun W . . . 2C 34
TN11: S'brne . . . 5H 13
TN15: Tonb, Bor G . . . 3G 13
Hurst Way TN13: S'oaks . . . 5J 9
Hurstwood La. TN4: Tun W . . . 5G 33
Hurstwood Pk. TN4: Tun W . . . 6H 33
Hyders Forge TN15: Plax . . . 5E 12
(not continuous)
Hythe Cl. TN4: S'bgh . . . 7J 27

I

Ide Hill Rd. TN8: Chid . . . 6A 14
TN14: Ide H . . . 2A 14
IGHTHAM . . . 6B 6
Ightham By-Pass TN15: Igh . . . 6A 6
IGHTHAM COMMON . . . 1K 11
Ightham Mote . . . 5J 11
Ightham Rd. TN11: S'brne . . . 7A 12
TN15: S'brne . . . 7A 12
Impala Gdns. TN4: Tun W . . . 3K 33
Inner London Rd. TN1: Tun W . . . 6J 33
Invicta Bus. Pk. TN15: Wro . . . 2G 7
Ironstones TN3: Lang G . . . 6D 32
Irving Ho. TN1: Tun W . . . 4K 33
Ismays Rd. TN15: Ivy H, Igh . . . 3K 11
Ives Rd. TN9: Tonb . . . 6H 21
IVY HATCH . . . 4K 11
Ivy Ho. La. TN13: Off, Dun G . . . 3D 2
Ivy La. TN3: Bell G . . . 5E 38

J

James Cl. TN11: Hdlw . . . 5K 19
Johnsons Ct. TN15: Seal . . . 6B 4
John Spare Ct. *TN4: Tun W* . . . *3J 33*
(off Whitefield Rd.)
John St. TN4: Tun W . . . 4J 33
Jubilee Cotts. TN14: S'oaks . . . 5H 3
Jubilee Cres. TN15: Igh . . . 6A 6
Jubilee Ri. TN15: Seal . . . 6B 4
Judd Rd. TN9: Tonb . . . 1K 27
Julians Cl. TN13: S'oaks . . . 5G 9
Julians Way TN13: S'oaks . . . 5G 9
Juniper Cl. TN4: S'bgh . . . 7B 28

K

Keel Gdns. TN4: S'bgh . . . 1G 33
Kelchers La. TN11: Gold G . . . 2K 23
Kelvin Cl. TN10: Tonb . . . 7B 18
Kemble Cl. TN2: Tun W . . . 2C 34
KEMSING . . . 2D 4
Kemsing Down Nature Reserve . . . 1B 4
Kemsing Heritage Cen. . . . 2D 4
Kemsing Rd. TN15: Wro, Kems'g . . . 1H 5
(not continuous)
Kemsing Station (Rail) . . . 4F 5
Kendal Cl. TN9: Tonb . . . 4A 22
Kendal Dr. TN9: Tonb . . . 5A 22
Kendal Pk. TN4: Tun W . . . 4G 33
Kennedy Gdns. TN13: S'oaks . . . 1J 9
Kennet Rd. TN10: Tonb . . . 2A 22
Kent & Sussex Crematorium
TN2: Tun W . . . 2K 37
KENT & SUSSEX HOSPITAL . . . 5J 33
Kent Cl. TN12: Pad W . . . 2G 31
Kentish Gdns. TN2: Tun W . . . 2G 37
Kent Rd. TN4: Tun W . . . 3J 33
Kenward Ct. TN11: Hdlw . . . 6J 19
Keswick Cl. TN9: Tonb . . . 5A 22
Keyes Gdns. TN9: Tonb . . . 1H 27
Keyworth Cl. TN12: Pad W . . . 2F 31
Kibbles La. TN4: S'bgh . . . 7G 27
Killick Cl. TN13: Dun G . . . 5E 2
Kiln La. TN11: Leigh . . . 6B 20
Kiln Way TN12: Pad W . . . 3G 31
Kincraig Dr. TN13: S'oaks . . . 1G 9
King George V Hill TN2: Tun W . . . 4A 34
Kingsmead Pk. TN12: Pad W . . . 2G 31
Kings Pk. TN2: Tun W . . . 6B 34
King's Rd. TN9: Tonb . . . 1A 28
Kings Standing Bus. Pk. TN2: Tun W . . . 7D 28
Kingstanding Way TN2: Tun W . . . 6D 28
Kings Toll Rd. TN2: Pem . . . 3K 35
Kingswood Cl. TN2: Tun W . . . 6A 34
Kingswood Rd. TN2: Tun W . . . 6A 34
TN13: Dun G . . . 5E 2
Kinnings Row TN9: Tonb . . . 5A 22
KIPPINGTON . . . 4G 9
Kippington Cl. TN13: S'oaks . . . 2F 9
Kippington Rd. TN13: S'oaks . . . 2G 9
Kirby Ct. TN3: Lang G . . . 6C 32
Kirkcourt TN13: S'oaks . . . 1G 9
Kirkdale Rd. TN1: Tun W . . . 5K 33
Knave Wood Rd. TN15: Kems'g . . . 2A 4
Knighton Rd. TN14: Otf . . . 1F 3
Knight Rd. TN10: Tonb . . . 1C 22
Knightsbridge Cl. TN4: Tun W . . . 4H 33
Knightsbridge Ct. TN1: Tun W . . . 3K 33
Knights Cl. TN2: Pem . . . 2H 35
Knights Pk. TN2: Tun W . . . 7D 28
(not continuous)
Knight's Pl. TN2: Pem . . . 2H 35
Knights Ridge TN2: Pem . . . 2H 35
Knights Way TN2: Tun W . . . 1D 34
Knole . . . 4A 10
Knole Cl. TN14: Weald . . . 4H 15
Knole La. TN13: S'oaks . . . 4J 9
Knole Pk. . . . 3K 9
Knole Rd. TN13: S'oaks . . . 1K 9
Knole Way TN13: S'oaks . . . 3J 9
Knotts Pl. TN13: S'oaks . . . 2G 9
Knowle Cl. TN3: Lang G . . . 6A 32
Knowle La. TN12: Brenc . . . 4J 31
Knowle Rd. TN12: Pad W, Brenc . . . 7J 31
Knowsley Way TN11: Hild . . . 1F 21

L

LADDINGFORD . . . 2K 25
Lady Amherst's Dr. TN14: Ide H . . . 2B 14
Lady's Gift Rd. TN4: S'bgh . . . 1H 33
Lady's Wlk. TN15: Ivy H, Igh . . . 2J 11
Lady Vane Cl. TN11: S'brne . . . 1A 18
LA Fitness . . . 5K 33
Lakeman Way TN4: Tun W . . . 2K 33
Lake Rd. TN4: Tun W . . . 5G 33
Lakeside TN2: Tun W . . . 3C 34
Lake Vw. Rd. TN13: S'oaks . . . 1G 9
Lambarde Dr. TN13: S'oaks . . . 1G 9
Lambarde Rd. TN13: S'oaks . . . 7G 3
Lambersart Cl. TN4: S'bgh . . . 7B 28
Lamberts Rd. TN2: Tun W . . . 1B 34
Lambert's Yd. TN9: Tonb . . . 6K 21
Lambourn Way TN2: Tun W . . . 1B 38
Lambs Bank TN9: Tonb . . . 1K 27
Lambs Mobile Home Pk. TN12: Pad W . . . 7G 25
Lampington Row TN3: Lang G . . . 6A 32
Landseer Cl. TN10: Tonb . . . 1C 22
Landway TN15: Seal . . . 5B 4
Landway, The TN15: Bor G . . . 5D 6
TN15: Kems'g . . . 2C 4
Langholm Rd. TN3: Lang G . . . 5B 32
LANGTON GREEN . . . 6B 32
Langton Ridge TN3: Lang G . . . 6D 32
Langton Rd. TN3: Lang G . . . 4B 32
TN3: R'hall, Lang G . . . 7A 32
TN4: Tun W, R'hall . . . 7A 32
Lansdowne Rd. TN1: Tun W . . . 5K 33
TN9: Tonb . . . 4K 21
TN13: S'oaks . . . 7K 3
Lansdowne Sq. TN1: Tun W . . . 5K 33
Lanthorne M. TN1: Tun W . . . 4K 33
Larch Cres. TN10: Tonb . . . 1A 22
Larch Gro. TN12: Pad W . . . 2F 31
Larkfield TN12: Five G . . . 1A 30
Larkfield Rd. TN13: Riv . . . 1C 8
Latters Flats TN11: Hdlw . . . 6J 19
Latymers TN11: Pens . . . 2B 26
Laurel Bank TN4: S'bgh . . . 2K 33
Laurel Rd. TN2: Tun W . . . 2B 34
Laurel Way TN2: Tun W . . . 2B 34
Lavender Ct. TN2: Tun W . . . 1G 37
Lavender Hill TN9: Tonb . . . 7A 22
Lawn Pk. TN13: S'oaks . . . 5H 9
Lawn Rd. TN9: Tonb . . . 7K 21
Lawns, The TN12: Brenc . . . 7H 31
Lawrence Rd. TN10: Tonb . . . 1C 22
Laxton Gdns. TN12: Pad W . . . 1E 30
Lealands Av. TN11: Leigh . . . 6C 20
Lealands Cl. TN3: Groom . . . 6C 36
Lea Rd. TN13: S'oaks . . . 5J 9
Leconfield Cl. TN9: Tonb . . . 1H 27
Leeds Ho. M. *TN11: Hdlw* . . . *6J 19*
(off Maidstone Rd.)
Lees Rd. ME18: Yald, Ladd . . . 1K 25
Leggs La. TN3: Speld, Lang G . . . 4A 32
Leicester Dr. TN2: Tun W . . . 2H 37
Leicester Sq. TN11: Pens . . . 2B 26
LEIGH . . . 6B 20
Leigh Rd. TN11: Hild . . . 2G 21
TN11: Leigh . . . 5F 21
Leigh Station (Rail) . . . 6B 20
Leighton Cl. TN4: Tun W . . . 2J 33
Lendon Rd. TN15: Bor G . . . 6D 6
Leneda Dr. TN2: Tun W . . . 2G 37
Lennard Rd. TN13: Dun G . . . 5E 2

Leonard Av. TN14: Otf 1H 3
Leslie Tew Ct. TN10: Tonb 2K 21
Le Temple Rd. TN12: Pad W 1H 31
Letter Box La. TN13: S'oaks 7J 9
Leybank TN11: Hild 3G 21
Leyburn Ct. TN9: Tonb 4A 22
(off Portman Pk.)
Lilley Cotts. TN11: Tude 7H 23
Lime Cl. TN3: Frant 6K 37
Lime Hill Rd. TN1: Tun W 5J 33
Lime Pit La. TN14: Dun G 2C 2
Lime Tree Cl. TN9: Tonb 5A 22
Lime Tree Wlk. TN13: S'oaks 3H 9
Linden Chase TN13: S'oaks 7H 3
Linden Cl. TN4: Tun W 7J 33
TN12: Pad W 2G 31
Linden Ct. TN10: Tonb 7K 17
Linden Gdns. TN2: Tun W 1H 37
Linden Pk. Rd. TN2: Tun W 7J 33
Linden Sq. TN13: Riv 7E 2
Lingfield Rd. TN15: Bor G 5F 7
Link Way TN2: Tun W 1C 34
Linnet Av. TN12: Pad W 3G 31
Lionel Rd. TN9: Tonb 7J 21
Lipscombe Rd. TN2: Tun W 3B 34
Liptraps La. TN2: Tun W 2B 34
LITTLE BAYHAM 5K 39
Lit. Boundes Cl. TN4: S'bgh 5G 27
Lit. Court Rd. TN13: S'oaks 2G 9
Littlefield TN11: Hdlw 6J 19
(off High St.)
Little Footway TN3: Lang G 6B 32
Lit. Julians Hill TN13: S'oaks 5G 9
Little Mallet TN3: Lang G 6A 32
LITTLE MILL 2D 24
Lit. Mount Sion TN1: Tun W 7J 33
Lit. Norman St. TN14: Ide H 7A 8
Littlewood TN13: S'oaks 7J 3
Loampits Cl. TN9: Tonb 4B 22
Lockington Ct. TN9: Tonb 1H 27
Lockside TN9: Tonb 5A 22
Locks Yd. TN13: S'oaks 3J 9
(off High St.)
Lodge La. TN3: Tun W 2C 36
Lodge Oak La. TN9: Tonb 1B 28
Lodge Rd. TN9: Tonb 5K 21
London Rd. TN1: Tun W 6J 33
TN4: S'bgh 4H 27
TN10: Tonb 3J 21
TN11: Hild 5C 16
TN13: Otf, Riv, Dun G 2D 2
TN13: S'oaks 1F 9
TN15: Addtn, W Mal, Off 3J 7
TN15: S'oaks 3A 16
TN15: Wro, W King, Bor G 1E 6
Lonewood Way TN11: Hdlw 4K 19
Long Barn Rd. TN14: Weald 4H 15
Longfield Rd. TN2: Tun W 1B 34
LONGFORD 5E 2
Longford Ct. TN13: Dun G 5E 2
Long Mdw. TN13: Riv 6D 2
Longmeads TN3: Lang G 5D 32
Longmead Stadium 2J 21
Long Mead Way TN10: Tonb 2K 21
Long Mill La. TN11: S'brne 5E 12
TN15: Bor G 5F 7
TN15: Plax 5E 12
Long Mill La. Crouch
TN15: Bor G 7G 7
Long Slip TN3: Lang G 6C 32
Longspring Wood TN13: S'oaks 7G 9
Longview Way TN2: Tun W 1B 34
Lonsdale Gdns. TN1: Tun W 5K 33
Lover's Wlk. TN9: Tonb 4A 22
LOWER BITCHET 4E 10
LOWER GREEN
Pembury 1H 35
Rusthall 4E 32
Lower Grn. TN11: Leigh 6B 20
Lwr. Green Rd. TN2: Pem 3H 35
TN3: Tun W, Speld 2D 32
TN4: R'hall 4E 32
LOWER HAYSDEN 7F 21
Lwr. Haysden La. TN11: Tonb 1E 26
Lower St. TN11: Hild 2A 20
Lowry, The TN9: Tonb 7K 21
Lucknow Rd. TN12: Pad W 7G 25
Lucks La. TN12: Pad W 6G 25
Lusted Rd. TN13: Dun G 5E 2
Lyle Pk. TN13: S'oaks 1H 9
Lyndhurst Dr. TN13: S'oaks 2E 8
Lynwood TN3: Groom 6C 36
Lyons Cres. TN9: Tonb 5A 22

M

Mabledon Rd. TN9: Tonb 7J 21
McDermott Rd. TN15: Bor G 5D 6
Macdonald Ct. TN12: Pad W 2G 31
Madeira Pk. TN2: Tun W 7J 33
Madison Way TN13: S'oaks 1F 9
Magnolia Cl. TN9: Tonb 1A 28
Maidstone Rd. TN2: Pem 1H 35
TN11: Hdlw 6J 19
TN12: Five G 2D 30
TN12: Mat 7D 30
TN12: Pad W 2F 31
TN13: Riv 7E 2
TN15: Seal 6C 4
TN15: Wro, Bor G 5D 6
Main Rd. TN14: Sund, Bras 2A 8
Major York's Rd. TN4: Tun W 6G 33
Maltings Cl. TN11: Hdlw 6J 19
Maltings, The TN11: Hdlw 6J 19
Malton Way TN2: Tun W 2D 34
Mann Sq. TN9: Tonb 1B 28
Manor Cl. TN4: Tun W 5G 33
Manor Farm Cotts. TN15: Igh 6J 5
Manor Gro. TN10: Tonb 4A 22
Manor Pk. TN4: Tun W 6G 33
Manor Rd. TN4: R'hall 5E 32
TN4: S'bgh 7G 27
Maple Cl. TN2: Tun W 1J 37
Market Pl. TN2: Tun W 7J 33
Market Sq. TN1: Tun W 5K 33
Market St. TN1: Tun W 7J 33
Marlborough Cl. TN4: Tun W 5G 33
Marlborough Cres. TN13: S'oaks 2E 8
Marshall Gdns. TN11: Hdlw 5J 19
Martin Hardie Way TN10: Tonb 2C 22
Martin's Dr. TN11: Leigh 7A 20
Martins Shaw TN13: Riv 7C 2
Marvillion Ct. TN12: E Peck 1F 25
Mary Burrows Gdns. TN15: Kems'g ...2D 4
Maryland Rd. TN2: Tun W 1B 38
Mary Magdalene Ho. TN9: Tonb 7K 21
Mascall's Ct. La. TN12: Pad W 4H 31
Mascall's Ct. Rd. TN12: Pad W 3G 31
Mascalls Pk. TN12: Pad W 3F 31
Masefield Way TN9: Tonb 7H 21
MATFIELD 7D 30
Matthews La. ME18: W Peck 1K 19
TN11: Hdlw 1K 19
Maycotts La. TN12: Mat 7D 30
Mayfield Rd. TN3: Frant, Mark C 7K 37
TN4: Tun W 5H 33
Maylam Ct. TN10: Tonb 3A 22
Meadow Bank TN11: Leigh 6B 20
Meadow Cl. TN13: S'oaks 1G 9
Meadow Hill Rd. TN1: Tun W 6K 33
Meadowlands TN15: Seal 5B 4
MEADOW LAWN 7J 21
Meadow Rd. TN1: Tun W 5J 33
TN3: Groom 5C 36
TN4: R'hall 5E 32
TN4: S'bgh 7H 27
TN9: Tonb 7J 21
Meadows, The TN11: Hild 3F 21
Meadow, The TN2: Pem 1H 35
Meadow Vw. ME18: Ladd 2K 25
TN13: Dun G 3D 2
Meads, The TN2: Tun W 7A 34
Meadway TN11: Hild 2G 21
Meadway, The TN13: S'oaks 7F 3
Medina Rd. TN1: Tun W 1A 22
Medway Mdws. TN12: E Peck 1G 25
Medway Rd. TN1: Tun W 4K 33
Medway Vw. TN11: Gold G 2A 24
Medway Wharf Rd. TN9: Tonb 6A 22
Mendip Wlk. TN2: Tun W 4B 34
Meopham Cotts. TN14: Weald 3H 15
Mercers TN3: Lang G 6C 32
Mercers Cl. TN12: Pad W 2E 30
Mercer St. TN1: Tun W 4K 33
Mereworth Rd. TN4: Tun W 3J 33
Merlewood TN13: S'oaks 1H 9
Merlin Cl. TN10: Tonb 2C 22
Merrion Cl. TN4: Tun W 2K 33
Merrion Way TN4: Tun W 2K 33
Merryfield Ct. TN9: Tonb 7J 21
Mersey Rd. TN10: Tonb 2K 21
Mews, The TN1: Tun W 6K 33
TN2: Pem 3G 35
TN13: S'oaks 1J 9
(Hartslands Rd.)
TN13: S'oaks 1G 9
(Hitchen Hatch La.)
Mid Comp Cotts. TN15: Bor G 6K 7
Middle Fld. TN4: R'hall 5E 32
Middlefield TN2: Pem 1J 35
Middle La. TN15: Seal 6B 4
Middle Rd. TN3: Bell G 5E 38
Middle Wlk. TN2: Tun W 1C 34
Middlings Ri. TN13: S'oaks 3F 9
Middlings, The TN13: S'oaks 4F 9
Middlings Wood TN13: S'oaks 3G 9
Midway, The TN4: Tun W 6F 33
Mile Oak Rd. TN12: Pad W, Brenc ...6J 31
Mill Bank TN9: Tonb 5A 22
Mill Cres. TN9: Tonb 5A 22
Mill La. TN9: Tonb 5A 22
TN11: Hild 7D 16
TN14: S'oaks 6J 3
TN15: Igh, Bor G 7B 6
TN15: Under 3D 16
Mill Pond Cl. TN14: S'oaks 6K 3
Mill Rd. TN13: Dun G 5E 2
Mills Cres. TN15: Seal 4B 4
Mill Stream Pl. TN9: Tonb 4B 22
Mill Vw. TN11: Hdlw 5H 19
Milton Dr. TN2: Tun W 2B 34
Milton Gdns. TN9: Tonb 1H 27
Milton Rd. TN13: Dun G 6E 2
Mimms Ter. TN12: Pad W 1G 31
Minters Orchard TN15: Bor G 5F 7
Mitre Ct. TN9: Tonb 5A 22
Moat Cl. TN13: Riv 7C 2
Moat Farm TN2: Tun W 3J 37
MODEST CORNER 7G 27
Molescroft Way TN9: Tonb 1H 27
Molyneux Cl. TN4: Tun W 5H 33
Molyneux Pk. Gdns. TN4: Tun W 5H 33
Molyneux Pk. Rd. TN4: Tun W 5G 33
Monks Wlk. TN9: Tonb 7K 21
Monkton Rd. TN15: Bor G 5D 6
Monson Colonnade TN1: Tun W 5K 33
(off Monson Rd.)
Monson Ho. TN1: Tun W 5K 33
Monson Rd. TN1: Tun W 5K 33
Monson Way TN1: Tun W 5K 33
(off Monson Rd.)
Montacute Gdns. TN4: Tun W 7H 33
Montacute Rd. TN2: Tun W 1J 37
Monteith Cl. TN3: Lang G 6C 32
Montfort Rd. TN15: Kems'g 2A 4
Montgomery Rd. TN13: Riv 2K 33
Montreal Rd. TN13: Riv 1E 8
Monypenny Cl. TN11: Hdlw 6H 19
Moor Rd. TN14: S'oaks 5H 3
Morants Ct. Rd. TN13: Dun G 3C 2
TN14: Dun G 3C 2
Morel Ct. TN13: S'oaks 7H 3
Morewood Cl. TN13: S'oaks 1F 9
Morewood Cl. Ind. Est. TN13: S'oaks ..1F 9
Morley Rd. TN9: Tonb 6B 22
Morley's Rd. TN14: Weald 4J 15
Mortley Cl. TN9: Tonb 5A 22
Mote Rd. TN11: S'brne 1H 17
TN15: Ivy H 7J 11
TN15: S'brne 1H 17
Mountain Cl. TN15: Wro 1D 6
(off West St.)
Mount Cl. TN13: S'oaks 1F 9
Mt. Edgecombe Rd. TN4: Tun W 6J 33
Mt. Ephraim TN1: Tun W 6H 33
Mt. Ephraim Rd. TN1: Tun W 5J 33
Mountfield TN15: Bor G 5E 6
Mountfield Ct. TN1: Tun W 6K 33
(off Mountfield Gdns.)
Mountfield Gdns. TN1: Tun W 6K 33
Mountfield Pk. TN9: Tonb 7A 22
Mountfield Rd. TN1: Tun W 6K 33
Mt. Harry Rd. TN13: S'oaks 1G 9
Mount Pleasant TN11: Hild 1F 21
TN12: Pad W 1F 31
TN14: Ide H 2A 14
Mt. Pleasant Av. TN1: Tun W 6K 33
Mt. Pleasant Ct. TN11: Hild 1F 21
Mt. Pleasant Rd. TN1: Tun W 6J 33
TN14: Weald 4H 15
Mount Sion TN1: Tun W 7J 33
(High St.)

Mount Sion TN1: Tun W 7J **33**
(Lit. Mount Sion)
Mulberry Cl. TN4: S'bgh 7B **28**
Munday Works Est. TN9: Tonb 6A **22**
Muskerry Ct. TN4: R'hall 5D **32**

N

Napier Rd. TN2: Tun W 7B **34**
Nellington Ct. TN4: R'hall 5D **32**
Nellington Rd. TN4: R'hall 4D **32**
Nelson Av. TN9: Tonb 6J **21**
Nelson Rd. TN2: Tun W 7B **34**
Nepicar Farm 3H **7**
Nepicar La. TN15: Wro 1G **7**
Nevill Ct. TN4: Tun W 7F **33**
Nevill Ga. TN2: Tun W 1K **37**
Nevill Lodge TN2: Tun W 4A **34**
Nevill Pk. TN4: Tun W, R'hall 6F **33**
Nevill Ridge TN4: R'hall 6F **33**
Nevill St. TN2: Tun W 7J **33**
Nevill Ter. TN2: Tun W 7H **33**
Newborough Ct. TN10: Tonb 1K **21**
Newbridge Pk. TN12: Pad W 6G **25**
New Camden Pk. TN2: Tun W 7A **34**
Newcomen Rd. TN4: Tun W 4J **33**
New Ct. TN9: Tonb 5A **22**
New England Rd. TN4: Tun W 2J **33**
New Ho. La. TN15: Wro 1C **6**
Newlands TN3: Lang G 6C **32**
Newlands Ri. TN4: Tun W 3J **33**
Newlands Rd. TN4: Tun W 3J **33**
Newlands Way TN4: Tun W 2K **33**
New Rd. TN12: Pad W 2G **31**
Newton Av. TN10: Tonb 7B **18**
Newton Gdns. TN12: Pad W 1F **31**
Newton Rd. TN1: Tun W 5K **33**
Newton Willows TN3: Groom 5C **36**
New Wlk. TN15: Wro 1D **6**
New Wharf Rd. TN9: Tonb 6K **21**
Nicolson Way TN13: S'oaks 7K **3**
Nightingale La. TN14: Ide H 7B **8**
(Back La.)
TN14: Ide H 1B **14**
(Yorks Hill Rd.)
Nightingale Rd. TN15: Kems'g 2K **3**
Nizels La. TN11: Hild 5B **16**
NOAH'S ARK **4D 4**
Noah's Ark TN15: Kems'g 3C **4**
Noble Tree Rd. TN11: Hild 1D **20**
Norfolk Rd. TN1: Tun W 7K **33**
TN9: Tonb 6J **21**
Norman Cl. TN15: Kems'g 2K **3**
Normanhurst Rd. TN15: Bor G 5E **6**
Norman Rd. TN1: Tun W 5K **33**
Norstead Gdns. TN4: S'bgh 1K **33**
Northcote Rd. TN9: Tonb 6K **21**
Nth. Down Cl. TN12: Pad W 2F **31**
Northdown Rd. TN15: Kems'g 2A **4**
Nth. Downs Bus. Pk. TN14: Dun G 1C **2**
Nth. Farm Ind. Est. TN2: Tun W 7B **28**
Nth. Farm La. TN2: Tun W 7C **28**
Nth. Farm Rd. TN2: Tun W 2A **34**
TN4: Tun W 2A **34**
Northfields TN3: Speld 1C **32**
Nth. Frith Pk. TN11: Hdlw 5C **18**
North St. TN2: Tun W 6A **34**
North Trench *TN10: Tonb* *1A 22*
(off Trench Rd.)
North Vw. Rd. TN14: S'oaks 6J **3**
Northwood Rd. TN10: Tonb 1K **21**
Norton Cres. TN10: Tonb 7K **17**
Norton Rd. TN4: S'bgh 7H **27**
Nortons Way TN12: Five G 1A **30**
Norwich Av. TN10: Tonb 2B **22**
Nottidge Rd. TN4: Tun W 1F **37**
Nursery Cl. TN10: Tonb 3B **22**
TN13: S'oaks 7J **3**
Nursery Pl. TN13: Riv 7D **2**
Nursery Rd. TN4: Tun W 1K **33**
TN12: Pad W 7F **25**
Nutfields TN15: Igh 1K **11**

O

Oak Av. TN13: S'oaks 6H **9**
Oak Cotts. TN11: Leigh 6A **20**
Oakdale Rd. TN4: Tun W 5H **33**
Oakdene Rd. TN13: S'oaks 7G **3**
Oak End Cl. TN4: S'bgh 6J **27**
Oakfield Ct. TN2: Tun W 6A **34**
Oakfield Ct. Rd. TN2: Tun W 6K **33**
Oakfields TN13: S'oaks 4H **9**
Oak Hill TN13: S'oaks 2G **9**
Oakhill Rd. TN13: S'oaks 2G **9**
Oaklands Rd. TN3: Groom 6B **36**
Oaklands Way TN11: Hild 2H **21**
Oak La. TN13: S'oaks 6F **9**
Oaklea Rd. TN12: Pad W 2F **31**
Oak Lodge TN13: S'oaks 2G **9**
Oakmead TN10: Tonb 1A **22**
Oak Rd. TN2: Tun W 2A **34**
TN12: Five G 1B **30**
Oak Sq. TN13: S'oaks 4J **9**
Oak Tree Cl. TN2: Tun W 1J **37**
Oak Warren TN13: S'oaks 7G **9**
Oakwood Dr. TN13: S'oaks 1H **9**
Oakwood Ri. TN2: Tun W 1C **34**
Oast Cl. TN2: Tun W 2B **34**
Oast Cotts. TN13: S'oaks 7G **3**
Oast La. TN10: Tonb 3J **21**
Oast Theatre 3J **21**
Odeon Cinema
Tunbridge Wells 1D **34**
Old Barn Cl. TN9: Tonb 7H **21**
TN15: Kems'g 2C **4**
OLDBURY **7K 5**
Oldbury Cl. TN15: Igh 7K **5**
Oldbury Cotts. TN15: Igh 6K **5**
Oldbury Hill 7J **5**
Oldbury La. TN15: Igh 6K **5**
Oldbury Vs. TN15: Igh 7K **5**
Oldbury Wood 1J **11**
Old Carriageway, The TN13: Riv 7C **2**
Old Church Rd. TN2: Pem 6H **29**
Old Cotts. TN15: Igh 7K **5**
Old Gdns. Cl. TN2: Tun W 2K **37**
Old Garden, The TN13: Riv 1C **8**
Old Hadlow Rd. TN10: Tonb 3C **22**
Old Kent Rd. TN12: Pad W 2F **31**
Old La. TN15: Igh 1K **11**
Old London Rd. TN10: Tonb 4A **22**
TN15: Wro 1D **6**
Old Otford Rd. TN14: Otf 2H **3**
TN14: S'oaks 3H **3**
Old Polhill TN14: Otf, Hals 1D **2**
(not continuous)
Old Rd. TN12: E Peck 1F **25**
Old Saw Mill, The TN15: Bor G 7H **7**
Old School Ct. TN13: S'oaks 7J **3**
Old Soar Manor 4F **13**
Old Soar Rd. TN15: Plax 5F **13**
Old Terry's Lodge Rd.
TN15: W King, Kems'g 1H **5**
Old Wlk., The TN14: Otf 2H **3**
Old Whetsted Rd. TN12: Five G 5F **25**
Orchard Bus. Cen. TN2: Tun W 1B **34**
TN9: Tonb 6C **22**
TN12: Five G 2C **30**
TN12: Pad W 7G **25**
Orchard Cl. TN2: Tun W 3B **34**
TN14: S'oaks 5J **3**
Orchard Dr. TN10: Tonb 2C **22**
Orchard Lea TN11: Hild 2H **21**
Orchard Pl. Bus. Pk. TN15: Off 6K **7**
Orchard Ri. TN3: Groom 6B **36**
Orchard Rd. TN12: E Peck 1G **25**
TN13: Riv 7E **2**
TN14: Otf 1F **3**
Orchard, The TN13: Dun G 6E **2**
Orchard Way TN15: Kems'g 2C **4**
Orchidhurst TN2: Tun W 2B **34**
Ospringe Pl. TN2: Tun W 3D **34**
OTFORD **1H 3**
Otford Heritage Cen. 1H **3**
Otford Rd. TN14: S'oaks 4H **3**
Otford Station (Rail) **1J 3**
Overdale TN14: Weald 4H **15**
Owletts All. *TN9: Tonb* *6K 21*
(off High St.)
Oxenhill Rd. TN15: Kems'g 2A **4**
Oxenhoath Rd. TN11: Hdlw 2G **19**
Ox Lea TN3: Lang G 6C **32**

P

Packhorse Rd. TN13: Riv 1C **8**
Paddock Cl. TN15: Bor G 6G **7**
Paddocks, The TN13: S'oaks 1K **9**
Paddock, The TN2: Pem 3G **35**
TN11: Hdlw 5J **19**
PADDOCK WOOD **1G 31**
Paddock Wood Bus. Cen. TN12: Pad W 1G **31**
Paddock Wood Distribution Cen.
TN12: Pad W 1H **31**
Paddock Wood Ind. Est. TN12: Pad W 1F **31**
Paddock Wood Station (Rail) **1G 31**
Paiges Farm Cl. TN14: Weald 4J **15**
Palmers Brook TN11: Hdlw 4K **19**
PALMER'S GREEN **7K 31**
Palmers Grn. La. TN12: Brenc 7K **31**
Pantiles, The TN2: Tun W 7J **33**
Parade, The TN15: Kems'g 2A **4**
Park Av. TN11: Hild 2H **21**
Park Cotts. TN11: Hdlw 4K **19**
Park Ct. TN4: Tun W 4J **33**
PARKER'S GREEN **1F 23**
Parkfield TN15: Seal, S'oaks 1A **10**
Pk. Grange Gdns. TN13: S'oaks 5J **9**
Pk. Hill Rd. TN14: Otf 2A **4**
Park Ho. TN13: S'oaks 7J **3**
Park Ho. Gdns. TN4: S'bgh 6J **27**
Parkland Cl. TN13: S'oaks 7J **9**
Park La. TN13: S'oaks 2J **9**
TN15: Kems'g 3C **4**
TN15: Seal, S'oaks 6C **4**
Park Pl. TN13: Riv 1D **8**
Park Rd. TN4: S'bgh 6J **27**
TN4: Tun W 4K **33**
TN11: Hdlw 2G **19**
Park St. TN2: Tun W 6A **34**
Parkview TN2: Tun W 5B **34**
Park Vs. TN11: Hdlw 5K **19**
Parkway TN10: Tonb 2B **22**
Parkwood Cl. TN2: Tun W 3A **34**
Parsonage Cl. TN4: R'hall 4D **32**
Parsonage Rd. TN4: R'hall 4D **32**
Patch, The TN13: Riv 7E **2**
Patience Cotts. TN14: Weald 4H **15**
Pavilion Gdns. TN13: S'oaks 2H **9**
Pavilion, The TN9: Tonb 6K **21**
Paynes Cotts. TN13: Dun G 3D **2**
Peach Hall TN10: Tonb 1A **22**
Pearson's Grn. La. TN12: Pad W 3J **31**
Pearson's Grn. Rd. TN12: Brenc 7K **31**
TN12: Pad W 4K **31**
Peckham Ct. TN12: E Peck 1F **25**
PECKHAM HURST **6K 13**
Peckham Hurst Rd.
ME18: S'brne, W Peck 6J **13**
TN11: S'brne 6J **13**
Peckham Wlk. Av. TN11: Plax 6B **12**
Pegasus Ct. TN4: Tun W 4K **33**
Pemble Cl. TN12: Five G 1A **30**
Pembroke M. TN13: S'oaks 3H **9**
Pembroke Rd. TN9: Tonb 6H **21**
TN13: S'oaks 3H **9**
PEMBURY **3H 35**
PEMBURY HOSPITAL 2F **35**
Pembury By-Pass TN2: Tun W, Pem 1E **34**
Pembury Cl. TN2: Pem 2H **35**
Pembury Grange TN2: Tun W 3E **34**
Pembury Gro. TN9: Tonb 7A **22**
(not continuous)
Pembury Hall Rd. TN2: Pem 5G **29**
TN11: Pem 5G **29**
Pembury Northern By-Pass TN2: Pem 2F **35**
Pembury Rd. TN2: Tun W 5A **34**
TN9: Tonb 7K **21**
TN11: Tun W, Tude 2B **28**
Pembury Walks TN2: Pem 6E **28**
TN11: Pem 6E **28**
Pendennis Rd. TN13: S'oaks 1H **9**
Penfolds Cl. TN10: Tonb 2A **22**
Pennine Wlk. TN2: Tun W 4B **34**
Pennington Mnr. TN4: S'bgh 6J **27**
Pennington Pl. TN4: S'bgh 6K **27**
Pennington Rd. TN4: S'bgh 6H **27**
Penn's Yd. TN2: Pem 3G **35**
Penruddocke Ho. TN10: Tonb 3A **22**
PENSHURST **2B 26**
Penshurst Place & Gardens 1B **26**
Penshurst Rd. TN3: Bidb 5A **26**
TN3: Speld, Pens 1A **32**
TN11: Leigh 6A **20**
TN11: Leigh, Pens 1A **26**
TN11: Pens 1A **32**
TN11: Pens, Bidb 5A **26**
Pen Way TN10: Tonb 2C **22**
Petersfield TN2: Pem 1J **35**

Petley Ct. Almshouses *TN9: Tonb* *7K* ***21***
(off Pembury Rd.)
Philpots La. TN11: Leigh, Hild 2A **20**
Pickmoss La. TN14: Otf 1G **3**
Pierce Mill La. TN11: Hdlw 2B **24**
Pikefish La. TN12: Pad W 6K **25**
Pilgrims Way TN13: Dun G 2D **2**
TN14: Dun G 2C **2**
TN14: Otf 1K **3**
TN15: Kems'g 1E **4**
TN15: Wro 1D **6**
(Battlefields Rd.)
TN15: Wro 1F **7**
(London Rd.)
Pilgrims Way Cotts.
TN15: Kems'g 2C **4**
Pilgrims Way E. TN14: Otf 1J **3**
Pilgrims Way W. TN13: Otf 2D **2**
TN14: Otf 1E **2**
Pillar Box La. TN11: Hdlw 1H **19**
Pillar Box Rd. TN15: Seal 7G **5**
Pinehurst TN14: S'oaks 6A **4**
Pine Needle La. TN13: S'oaks 1H **9**
Pine Ridge TN10: Tonb 1K **21**
Pine Tree La. TN15: Ivy H 3J **11**
Pine Vw. TN15: Bor G 5G **7**
Pinewood Av. TN14: S'oaks 6K **3**
Pinewood Cl. TN12: Pad W 2F **31**
Pinewood Ct. TN4: S'bgh 7J **27**
Pinewood Gdns. TN4: S'bgh 7J **27**
Pinewood Rd. TN2: Tun W 4B **34**
Pink All. *TN2: Tun W* *7J* ***33***
(off Nevill St.)
Pinkham TN12: E Peck 2G **25**
Pinkham Gdns. TN12: E Peck 1G **25**
Pinnacles Cl. TN10: Tonb 2A **22**
Pippin Rd. TN12: E Peck 1F **25**
PITTSWOOD **6E** 18
Pittswood TN11: Hdlw 6F **19**
Pittswood Cotts. TN11: Hdlw 6E **18**
Pixot Hill TN12: Brenc 7H **31**
Plane Wlk. TN10: Tonb 7A **18**
Platt Comn. TN15: Bor G 5G **7**
Platt Ind. Est. TN15: Bor G 4F **7**
Platt Mill Cl. TN15: Bor G 5F **7**
Platt Mill Ter. TN15: Bor G 5F **7**
PLAXTOL **5C** 12
Plaxtol La. TN15: Plax 5A **12**
PLAXTOL SPOUTE **5D** 12
Plough Hill TN15: Bor G 1D **12**
Plummers Cft. TN13: Dun G 6E **2**
Plymouth Dr. TN13: S'oaks 2J **9**
Plymouth Pk. TN13: S'oaks 2J **9**
Pocket Hill TN13: S'oaks 6G **9**
Point Cnr. TN11: S'brne 1D **18**
Polesden Rd. TN2: Tun W 7B **34**
Polhill TN14: Hals 1C **2**
Polley Cl. TN2: Pem 2H **35**
Pond La. TN15: Ivy H 3G **11**
Pontoise Cl. TN13: S'oaks 7F **3**
Poona Rd. TN1: Tun W 7K **33**
Poppy Mdw. TN12: Pad W 3G **31**
Portland Cl. TN10: Tonb 7B **18**
Portman Pk. TN9: Tonb 4A **22**
Postern Ind. Est. TN9: Tonb 5B **22**
Postern La. TN11: Tonb 5B **22**
Post Office Sq. TN1: Tun W 6J **33**
Potash La. TN15: Bor G 6G **7**
Pound Ho. *TN11: Hdlw* *6J* ***19***
(off Maidstone Rd.)
Pound La. TN13: S'oaks 2J **9**
Pound Rd. TN12: E Peck 1E **24**
POUNDSBRIDGE **1A** 32
Poundsbridge Hill
TN3: Ford, Pens 2A **32**
TN11: Pens 2A **32**
Poundsbridge La. TN11: Pens 6A **26**
Pound, The TN12: E Peck 1F **25**
Pounsley Rd. TN13: Dun G 6E **2**
Powder Mill Cl. TN4: S'bgh 1A **34**
Powder Mill La.
TN4: Tun W, S'bgh 2J **33**
TN11: Leigh 5C **20**
(Hildenborough Rd.)
TN11: Leigh 5F **21**
(Leigh Rd.)
POWDER MILLS **5G** 21
Prall's La. TN12: Mat 6E **30**
Preston Rd. TN9: Tonb 6J **21**
Priestley Dr. TN10: Tonb 7B **18**
Primrose Wlk. TN12: Pad W 3G **31**
Princes St. TN2: Tun W 6A **34**
Priory Gro. TN9: Tonb 7K **21**
Priory Rd. TN9: Tonb 7K **21**
Priory St. TN9: Tonb 7K **21**
Priory Wlk. TN9: Tonb 7K **21**
Prospect Pk. TN4: S'bgh 7H **27**
Prospect Rd. TN2: Tun W 6K **33**
TN4: S'bgh 7H **27**
TN13: S'oaks 1J **9**
Providence Cotts. *TN3: Groom* *5C* ***36***
(off Corseley Rd.)
Prudence Cotts. TN14: Weald 4H **15**
Pudding La. TN15: Seal 6B **4**
Purcell Av. TN10: Tonb 1D **22**
Putlands Sports & Leisure Cen. 3F 31
Puttenden Rd. TN11: S'brne 2D **18**
Pychers Pl. TN2: Pem 3H **35**

Q

Quaker Cl. TN13: S'oaks 1K **9**
Quakers Hall La. TN13: S'oaks 7J **3**
Quantock Cl. TN2: Tun W 4B **34**
Quarry Bank TN9: Tonb 1J **27**
Quarry Cotts. TN13: S'oaks 1F **9**
Quarry Gdns. TN9: Tonb 7J **21**
Quarry Hill TN15: S'oaks 1K **9**
Quarry Hill Pde. TN9: Tonb 7K **21**
Quarry Hill Rd. TN9: Tonb 1J **27**
(not continuous)
TN15: Bor G 6D **6**
Quarry Ri. TN9: Tonb 1J **27**
Quarry Rd. TN1: Tun W 4K **33**
Queens Dr. TN14: S'oaks 5J **3**
Queen's Gdns. TN4: Tun W 3K **33**
Queen's Rd. TN4: Tun W 4J **33**
QUEEN STREET **7K** 25
Queen St. TN12: Pad W 3J **31**
Quincewood Gdns. TN10: Tonb 7K **17**

R

Raeburn Cl. TN10: Tonb 1C **22**
Ragge Way TN15: Seal 5B **4**
Railway App. TN9: Tonb 6K **21**
RAMSLYE **1G** 37
Ramslye Rd. TN4: Tun W 1F **37**
Randall Hill Rd. TN15: Wro 1D **6**
Rankine Rd. TN2: Tun W 2B **34**
Raphael Ct. TN11: Hild 7F **17**
Ravenswood Av. TN2: Tun W 3A **34**
Rear, The *TN2: Tun W* *7J* ***33***
(off Pantiles, The)
Rectory Dr. TN3: Bidb 5E **26**
Rectory La. TN13: S'oaks 4H **9**
TN15: Igh 7A **6**
Red Ho. Cotts. TN13: S'oaks 3J **9**
Redlands Rd. TN13: S'oaks 2F **9**
Redleaf Cl. TN2: Tun W 3B **34**
Redpoll Wlk. TN12: Pad W 3G **31**
Redwell Cotts. TN15: Igh 1A **12**
Redwell La. TN15: Igh 1K **11**
Redwings La. TN2: Pem 7H **29**
Redwood Pk. TN12: Five G 3A **30**
Reeds La. TN11: S'brne 1C **18**
Regency Hall TN2: Tun W 7J **33**
Regent Pl. TN2: Tun W 6B **34**
Regina Ct. TN4: Tun W 5H **33**
Rembrandt Cl. TN10: Tonb 1C **22**
Retreat, The TN13: S'oaks 3H **9**
Reynolds Cl. TN10: Tonb 1C **22**
Reynolds La. TN4: Tun W 2H **33**
Ribston Gdns. TN12: Pad W 1E **30**
Richardson Rd. TN4: Tun W 3J **33**
Richmond Pl. TN2: Tun W 1K **37**
Riddlesdale Av. TN4: Tun W 3J **33**
Ridgelands TN3: Bidb 4E **26**
Ridge, The TN3: Groom 6A **36**
Ridgeway TN2: Pem 2H **35**
Ridgeway Cres. TN10: Tonb 3B **22**
Ridgewaye, The TN4: S'bgh 7J **27**
Ridgeway, The TN10: Tonb 2A **22**
Ridgy Fld. Cl. TN15: Wro 2E **6**
Riding La. TN11: Hild 1F **21**
Riding Pk. TN11: Hild 7F **17**
Ridings, The TN2: Tun W 3D **34**
TN12: Pad W 1G **31**
Riggs Way TN15: Wro 1D **6**
Ringden Av. TN12: Pad W 3E **30**
Rings Hill TN11: Hild 1D **20**
Rise, The TN13: S'oaks 7J **9**
River Cen., The *TN9: Tonb* *6A* ***22***
(off Medway Wharf Rd.)
River Ct. TN13: Riv 7E **2**
Riverdale Est. TN9: Tonb 7B **22**
RIVERHEAD **7E** 2
Riverhead M. TN13: Riv 1E **8**
River Hill TN15: S'oaks 1K **15**
Riverhill House & Gardens 2A 16
River Lawn Rd. TN9: Tonb 6K **21**
River Pde. TN13: Riv 7E **2**
Riverside Ct. TN9: Tonb 6A **22**
Riverside Retail Pk. TN14: S'oaks 4J **3**
River Wlk. TN9: Tonb 6K **21**
Robinwood Dr. TN15: Seal 4B **4**
Robyns Way TN13: S'oaks 7F **3**
Rochdale Rd. TN1: Tun W 4A **34**
Rochester Rd. TN10: Tonb 3B **22**
Rockdale TN13: S'oaks 3H **9**
Rockdale Gdns. TN13: S'oaks 3H **9**
Rockdale Pleasance TN13: S'oaks 4H **9**
Rockdale Rd. TN13: S'oaks 3J **9**
Rock Rd. TN15: Bor G 5D **6**
Rock Villa Rd. TN1: Tun W 5J **33**
Rodmell Rd. TN2: Tun W 7J **33**
Rodney Av. TN10: Tonb 3C **22**
Roedean Rd. TN2: Tun W 1J **37**
Rogues Hill TN11: Pens 2B **26**
Roman Ct. TN15: Bor G 5D **6**
ROMFORD **2K** 35
Romford Rd. TN2: Pem 2H **35**
TN2: Mat 7B **30**
Romney Way TN10: Tonb 2C **22**
Ronley Ct. *TN13: S'oaks* *6J* ***3***
(off Hillingdon Av.)
Rookdean TN13: Riv 7C **2**
Rookley Cl. TN2: Tun W 7B **34**
Rooks Hill TN15: Under 7E **10**
(not continuous)
Roopers TN3: Speld 2C **32**
Roper's Ga. TN4: Tun W 1G **37**
Rosecroft Pk. TN3: Lang G 5C **32**
Rosefield TN13: S'oaks 2G **9**
Rosehill Wlk. TN1: Tun W 6J **33**
Rose St. TN9: Tonb 7A **22**
Rossdale TN2: Tun W 4A **34**
Rossetti Gdns. TN2: Tun W 1K **37**
Rother Rd. TN10: Tonb 2K **21**
ROUGHWAY **7F** 13
Roughway La. TN11: Rough, S'brne 7E **12**
Roundhill Rd. TN2: Tun W 1B **38**
Rowan Cl. TN12: Pad W 3F **31**
Rowan Shaw TN10: Tonb 1B **22**
Rowan Tree Rd. TN2: Tun W 1G **37**
Rowdow TN14: Otf 1K **3**
Rowley Hill TN2: Pem 7H **29**
Royal Av. TN9: Tonb 7A **22**
Royal Chase TN4: Tun W 5H **33**
Royal Ri. TN9: Tonb 7A **22**
ROYAL TUNBRIDGE WELLS **7J** 33
Royal Tunbridge Wells Bus. Pk.
TN2: Tun W 7C **28**
Royal Tunbridge Wells District Indoor Bowls Club 7C 34
Royal Victoria Hall 7J 27
Royal Victoria Pl. TN1: Tun W 5K **33**
Royal W. Kent Av. TN10: Tonb 3B **22**
Ruscombe Cl. TN4: S'bgh 6H **27**
Rushetts TN3: Lang G 5B **32**
Rushlye Cl. TN3: Bell G 5D **38**
Rushmere Ct. TN15: Igh 5B **6**
Rushymead TN15: Kems'g 3C **4**
Russett Rd. TN12: E Peck 1F **25**
RUSTHALL **5E** 32
Rusthall Grange TN4: R'hall 5F **33**
Rusthall Pk. TN4: Tun W, R'hall 5F **33**
(not continuous)
Rusthall Pl. TN4: R'hall 6F **33**
Rusthall Rd. TN4: R'hall 5E **32**
Rustwick TN4: R'hall 5F **33**
Rutherford Way TN10: Tonb 7B **18**
Rycroft La. TN14: S'oaks 1E **14**
Rydal Cl. TN4: Tun W 4G **33**
Rydal Dr. TN4: Tun W 4G **33**
Ryders TN3: Lang G 6C **32**
Ryecroft Rd. TN14: Otf 2G **3**
Rye La. TN14: Otf, Dun G 5F **3**
Rye Lane Pottery 5F 3
Ryewood Cotts. TN14: Dun G 5F **3**
Rymers Cl. TN2: Tun W 2B **34**

S

Sackville Cl. TN13: S'oaks 7H **3**
St Andrew's Cl. TN12: Pad W 2G **31**
St Andrews Ct. TN4: S'bgh 7J **27**
St Andrew's Pk. Rd. TN4: S'bgh 7J **27**
St Andrew's Rd. TN12: Pad W 2G **31**
St Augustine Ho. *TN9: Tonb* *7K **21***
(off Priory Rd.)
St Barnabas Cl. TN1: Tun W 4A **34**
St Bernards Rd. TN10: Tonb 1A **22**
St Botolph's Av. TN13: S'oaks 2G **9**
St Botolph's Rd. TN13: S'oaks 2H **9**
St David's Rd. TN4: Tun W 2K **33**
St Edith Cotts. TN15: Kems'g 1K **5**
St Edith's Farm Cotts. TN15: Kems'g 3D **4**
St Edith's Rd. TN15: Kems'g 3C **4**
St Georges Ct. TN15: Wro 1D **6**
St George's M. TN9: Tonb 7K **21**
St George's Pk. TN2: Tun W 2H **37**
St George's Rd. TN13: S'oaks 7H **3**
St Hildas TN15: Plax 5D **12**
St James Cl. TN10: Tonb 7B **18**
St James Ct. TN1: Tun W 5K **33**
St James' Pk. TN1: Tun W 4A **34**
St James Rd. TN1: Tun W 4K **33**
TN13: S'oaks 7H **3**
ST JOHN'S
Sevenoaks 7J **3**
Tunbridge Wells 4J **33**
St John's Ct. TN13: S'oaks 7J **3**
St John's Hill TN13: S'oaks 6J **3**
St John's Pk. TN4: Tun W 1J **33**
St John's Rd. TN4: S'bgh 1J **33**
TN4: Tun W 3J **33**
TN13: S'oaks 6H **3**
St Julian Rd. TN15: S'oaks, Under 1A **16**
St Lawrence Av. TN4: Bidb 5F **27**
St Luke's Rd. TN4: Tun W 3K **33**
St Mark's Rd. TN2: Tun W 2H **37**
St Marys Cl. ME18: Ladd 3K **25**
TN15: Bor G 5G **7**
St Mary's Dr. TN13: Riv 1E **8**
St Mary's La. TN3: Speld 1C **32**
ST MARYS PLATT 5G **7**
St Mary's Rd. TN9: Tonb 1K **27**
TN15: Wro 2E **6**
St Michaels Ct. TN11: Hild 7F **17**
St Michael's Dr. TN14: Otf 1K **3**
St Michael's Rd. TN4: Tun W 3K **33**
St Nicholas Ct. *TN13: S'oaks* *3H **9***
(off Lime Tree Wlk.)
St Nicholas Dr. TN13: S'oaks 4H **9**
St Paul's Cl. TN10: Tonb 2B **22**
St Pauls Ct. TN4: R'hall 5E **32**
St Paul's St. TN4: R'hall 5E **32**
St Peters St. TN2: Tun W 6A **34**
St Philips Ct. TN2: Tun W 3B **34**
St Stephens Ct. TN1: Tun W 4K **33**
St Stephen's St. TN9: Tonb 7K **21**
St Vincent's La. ME19: Addtn 3K **7**
Salamons Rd. TN4: R'hall 5E **32**
Salisbury Cl. TN10: Tonb 2B **22**
Salisbury Rd. TN3: Lang G 6B **32**
TN4: Tun W 1A **34**
TN10: Tonb 3B **22**
Salmans La. TN11: Pens 2A **26**
Sanderson Way TN9: Tonb 6B **22**
TN11: Tonb 6C **22**
Sandhurst Av. TN2: Pem 3J **35**
Sandhurst Cl. TN2: Tun W 2A **34**
Sandhurst Pk. TN2: Tun W 2A **34**
Sandhurst Rd. TN2: Tun W 2A **34**
Sandilands TN13: Riv 7D **2**
Sandown Cl. TN2: Tun W 3D **34**
Sandown Gro. TN2: Tun W 3D **34**
SANDOWN PARK 3D **34**
Sandown Pk. TN2: Tun W 4D **34**
(not continuous)
Sandringham M. TN4: Tun W 4J **33**
Sandrock Ho. TN2: Tun W 5B **34**
Sandrock Rd. TN2: Tun W 5A **34**
Sandy La. ME19: Addtn 3K **7**
ME19: Addtn 3K **7**
TN13: S'oaks 1J **9**
TN15: Ivy H, Igh 3K **11**
Sandy Ridge TN15: Bor G 5E **6**
Saunders Rd. TN4: Tun W 1G **37**
Saville Cl. TN10: Tonb 7B **18**
Saxbys Rd. TN15: Seal 7F **5**
Saxby Wood TN11: Leigh 6B **20**
Saxon Cl. TN14: Otf 2F **3**
Scabharbour La. TN11: Hild 7J **15**
Scabharbour Rd. TN14: Weald, Hild 4J **15**
School App. TN15: Bor G 5E **6**
School La. TN11: Hdlw 5J **19**
TN11: Plax, S'brne 6C **12**
TN15: Plax 6C **12**
TN15: Seal 6B **4**
School Ri. TN2: Tun W 1H **37**
Scott Rd. TN9: Tonb 7H **21**
Scotts Way TN2: Tun W 2G **37**
TN13: Riv 7E **2**
Seabrook Rd. TN10: Tonb 3J **21**
SEAL 6B **4**
SEAL CHART 1E **10**
Sealcroft Cotts. TN15: Seal 4B **4**
Seal Dr. TN15: Seal 6B **4**
Seal Hollow Rd. TN13: S'oaks 2J **9**
Seal Rd. TN14: S'oaks 6J **3**
Selby's Cotts. TN11: Hild 3F **21**
Sellbourne Pk. TN3: Frant 6A **38**
Senlac Pl. *TN3: Groom* *5C **36***
(off Meadow Rd.)
Sennocke Ct. TN13: S'oaks 3H **9**
Serpentine Ct. TN13: S'oaks 7K **3**
Serpentine Rd. TN13: S'oaks 1J **9**
Seven Mile La. TN15: Wro 4K **7**
(not continuous)
SEVENOAKS 3J **9**
Sevenoaks Bus. Cen. TN14: S'oaks 6J **3**
Sevenoaks By-Pass TN14: S'oaks, Riv 1C **8**
SEVENOAKS COMMON 7H **9**
SEVENOAKS HOSPITAL 6J **3**
Sevenoaks Leisure Cen. 3J **9**
Sevenoaks Mus. & Art Gallery *3J 9*
(in Library)
Sevenoaks Rd. TN14: S'oaks, Otf 1H **3**
TN15: Bor G 5D **6**
TN15: Seal, Igh 1H **11**
(not continuous)
Sevenoaks Station (Rail) 2G **9**
SEVENOAKS WEALD 4H **15**
Sevenoaks Wildfowl Reserve 6F **3**
Sevenoaks Wildfowl Reserve Vis. Cen. 6F **3**
Severn Cl. TN10: Tonb 2A **22**
Shab Hall Cotts. TN13: Dun G 3C **2**
Shaftesbury Rd. TN4: Tun W 3J **33**
Shakespeare Rd. TN9: Tonb 7H **21**
Shambles, The TN13: S'oaks 3J **9**
Shandon Cl. TN2: Tun W 5A **34**
Shaw, The TN2: Tun W 7A **34**
SHEET HILL 3D **12**
Sheet Hill TN15: Plax 3B **12**
Sheffield Rd. TN4: S'bgh 6H **27**
Sheilings, The TN15: Seal 5B **4**
Shelton Cl. TN10: Tonb 2A **22**
Shenden Cl. TN13: S'oaks 5J **9**
Shenden Way TN13: S'oaks 6J **9**
Shepherds Wlk. TN2: Tun W 5B **34**
Sherborne Cl. TN2: Tun W 7B **34**
Sherbourne Gro. TN15: Kems'g 2C **4**
Sherenden Pk. TN11: Gold G 2A **24**
(not continuous)
Sherenden Rd. TN11: Tude 6G **23**
Sheridan Ct. TN11: Hild 3H **21**
Shernfold Pk. TN3: Frant 7A **38**
Sherwood Cotts. TN2: Tun W 3C **34**
SHERWOOD PARK 3B **34**
Sherwood Pk. TN2: Tun W 4C **34**
Sherwood Pl. TN3: Lang G 6A **32**
Sherwood Rd. TN2: Tun W 3B **34**
Sherwood Way TN2: Tun W 3B **34**
Shinecroft TN14: Otf 1G **3**
SHIPBOURNE 1A **18**
Shipbourne Rd. TN10: Tonb 4A **22**
TN11: Tonb 3B **18**
Shires, The TN12: Pad W 1G **31**
Shirley Cotts. TN4: Tun W 4J **33**
Shirley Gdns. TN4: R'hall 5E **32**
Shirley Gro. TN4: R'hall 4E **32**
Shoreham La. TN13: S'oaks, Riv 7F **3**
Shoreham Rd. TN14: S'ham, Otf 1J **3**
Shorehill Ct. TN15: Kems'g 2B **4**
Shorehill La. TN15: Kems'g, Knat 1B **4**
(not continuous)
Short La. TN15: Igh 1K **11**
Showfields Rd. TN2: Tun W 1H **37**
Shrublands Ct. TN2: Tun W 5A **34**
TN9: Tonb 5B **22**
Sidney Cl. TN2: Tun W 2G **37**
Sidney Gdns. TN14: Otf 1J **3**
Sign Post Fld. TN11: Gold G 2A **24**
Silk Mills Cl. TN14: S'oaks 6J **3**
Silver Cl. TN9: Tonb 2K **27**
Silverdale La. TN4: Tun W 2K **33**
Silverdale Rd. TN4: Tun W 3K **33**
Silverhurst Dr. TN10: Tonb 1A **22**
Silwood Cl. TN2: Tun W 2C **34**
Simmonds Ct. TN4: R'hall 5D **32**
Sion Wlk. *TN1: Tun W* *7J **33***
(off Mount Sion)
Sir David's Pk. TN4: S'bgh 7G **27**
Siskin Gdns. TN12: Pad W 3G **31**
Six Bells La. TN13: S'oaks 4J **9**
Skinner's Ter. TN9: Tonb 7K **21**
Slade, The TN9: Tonb 5K **21**
Smithers Cl. TN11: Hdlw 5J **19**
Smithers Ct. TN12: E Peck 1G **25**
Smythe Cl. TN4: S'bgh 5G **27**
Snipe Cl. TN2: Pem 1J **35**
SNOLL HATCH 2E **24**
Snoll Hatch Rd. TN12: E Peck 2E **24**
Solefields Rd. TN13: S'oaks 6H **9**
Soleoak Dr. TN13: S'oaks 5H **9**
SOMERHILL 2D **28**
Somerhill Rd. TN9: Tonb 7B **22**
Somerset Rd. TN4: Tun W 3J **33**
Somerset Vs. *TN3: Groom* *5C **36***
(off Corseley Rd.)
Somerville Gdns. TN4: Tun W 5H **33**
SOUTHBOROUGH 7J **27**
Southborough Ct. TN4: S'bgh 7H **27**
South Farm La. TN3: Tun W 3B **36**
Southfield Rd. TN4: Tun W 3J **33**
Southfields TN3: Speld 2C **32**
Southfields Way TN4: S'bgh 1K **33**
South Gro. TN1: Tun W 7J **33**
South Pk. TN13: S'oaks 3H **9**
South Trench TN10: Tonb 2A **22**
South Vw. Rd. TN4: Tun W 1K **33**
Southwood Av. TN4: Tun W 3J **33**
Southwood Rd. TN4: R'hall 4D **32**
Sovereign Way TN9: Tonb 6A **22**
Spa Cl. TN11: Hdlw 5K **19**
Spa Ind. Pk. TN2: Tun W 1C **34**
SPELDHURST 1C **32**
Speldhurst Hill TN3: Speld 2C **32**
Speldhurst Rd. TN3: Lang G 6A **32**
TN4: Tun W, S'bgh 1F **33**
Spencer M. *TN1: Tun W* *7J **33***
(off Berkeley Rd.)
Spencers Cotts. TN15: Bor G 5D **6**
Speyside TN10: Tonb 2K **21**
Spinney, The TN9: Tonb 1J **27**
Springfield Pl. *TN3: Groom* *5C **36***
(off Corseley Rd.)
Springfield Rd. TN3: Groom 5C **36**
TN4: S'bgh 7H **27**
Spring Gdns. TN4: R'hall 5D **32**
Springhead TN2: Tun W 4B **34**
Spring Head Rd. TN15: Kems'g 2B **4**
Spring La. TN3: Bidb 5E **26**
TN15: Igh 7K **5**
Springshaw Cl. TN13: Riv 1D **8**
Springshaw Ct. TN2: Tun W 3B **34**
Springwell Rd. TN9: Tonb 7K **21**
Springwood Pk. TN11: Tonb 5B **18**
Spurway, The TN4: Tun W 7F **33**
Square, The TN11: Hdlw 6J **19**
TN11: Leigh 6B **20**
TN13: Riv 7E **2**
Squirrel Way TN2: Tun W 4C **34**
Stable Ct. TN13: S'oaks 4J **9**
Stabledene Way TN2: Pem 3H **35**
Stable Yd. TN15: Kems'g 2C **4**
Stacey Rd. TN10: Tonb 3H **21**
Stafford Rd. TN2: Tun W 5C **34**
TN9: Tonb 5K **21**
Stafford Way TN13: S'oaks 5J **9**
Stag Rd. TN2: Tun W 1B **34**
Stag Theatre & Cinema 3H **9**
Stainer Rd. TN10: Tonb 1C **22**
Stairfoot La. TN13: Riv 7C **2**
Stair Rd. TN10: Tonb 3D **22**
Staleys Acre TN15: Bor G 5D **6**
Staleys Rd. TN15: Bor G 5C **6**
STALLIONS GREEN 4G **19**
Standen St. TN4: Tun W 4J **33**
Stanham Rd. TN2: Pem 3J **35**
Stanhope Rd. TN1: Tun W 4A **34**
Stanhope Way TN13: Riv 7D **2**

Stan La. ME18: W Peck .6K **13**
Stanley Rd. TN1: Tun W .4K **33**
Stapleford Ct. TN13: S'oaks .2F **9**
Star Hill Rd. TN14: Dun G .1A **2**
Station App. TN1: Tun W .6J **33**
TN12: Pad W .1G **31**
TN15: Bor G .5D **6**
Station Ct. *TN15: Bor G .4D 6*
(off Station App.)
Station Pde. TN13: S'oaks .2G **9**
Station Rd. TN3: Groom .5C **36**
TN12: Pad W .1F **31**
TN13: Dun G .5E **2**
TN14: Otf .1H **3**
TN15: Bor G .5D **6**
Steers Pl. TN11: Hdlw .4J **19**
Stenning Ct. *TN10: Tonb .3A 22*
(off Uridge Cres.)
Stephen's Rd. TN4: Tun W .3J **33**
Stewart Rd. TN4: Tun W .2A **34**
Still La. TN4: S'bgh .6H **27**
Stockenbury TN12: E Peck .1F **25**
STOCKLAND GREEN .7E **26**
Stockland Grn. Rd. TN3: S'bgh .1D **32**
STOCKS GREEN .2D **20**
Stocks Grn. Rd. TN11: Hild .2D **20**
Stone Ct. La. TN2: Pem .1J **35**
Stone Ho. Fld. TN15: Bor G .5F **7**
STONE STREET .3H **11**
Stone St. TN1: Tun W .5K **33**
Stone St. Rd. TN15: Ivy H, Seal .1E **10**
Stonewall Pk. Rd. TN3: Lang G .6B **32**
Stonewood Cl. TN4: Tun W .1J **33**
Stour Cl. TN10: Tonb .2K **21**
Stratford St. TN1: Tun W .4A **34**
Strawberry Cl. TN2: Tun W .2G **37**
Strawberry Hill TN3: Tun W .4F **37**
Strawberry Va. TN9: Tonb .7A **22**
Stream Side TN10: Tonb .7B **18**
Street, The TN15: Igh .6B **6**
TN15: Plax .5C **12**
Strettit Gdns. TN12: E Peck .2F **25**
Stuart Cl. TN2: Tun W .2H **37**
Stumble Hill TN11: S'brne .2A **18**
STYANTS BOTTOM .7H **5**
Styants Bottom Rd. TN15: Seal .6H **5**
Styles Ct. TN12: Pad W .1F **31**
Suffolk Way TN13: S'oaks .3J **9**
Sullivan Rd. TN10: Tonb .1C **22**
Summerhill Av. TN4: S'bgh .7H **27**
Summervale Rd. TN4: Tun W .1F **37**
Sundridge Rd. TN14: Dun G .5A **2**
Sunhill Ct. TN2: Pem .3G **35**
Sunnyside Rd. TN4: R'hall .5E **32**
Sunrise Cotts. TN13: S'oaks .7F **3**
Surrey Cl. TN2: Tun W .2H **37**
Sussex Cl. TN2: Tun W .1A **38**
Sussex M. TN2: Tun W .7J **33**
Sussex Rd. TN9: Tonb .7J **21**
Sutherland Rd. TN1: Tun W .6K **33**
Swaffield Rd. TN13: S'oaks .7J **3**
Swallow Dr. TN2: Tun W .3D **34**
Swanland Dr. TN9: Tonb .1H **27**
Swanmead Way TN9: Tonb .5B **22**
Swanton La. ME18: S'brne, W Peck .6H **13**
Swanton Rd. ME18: W Peck .6K **13**
SWANTON VALLEY .5K **13**
Swanzy Rd. TN14: S'oaks .5J **3**
Sweeps Hill Cl. TN2: Pem .2H **35**
Swift Ct. TN15: Seal .6C **4**
Sycamore Cotts. TN2: Pem .3G **35**
Sycamore Gdns. TN12: Pad W .3F **31**
Sychem La. TN12: Five G .1A **30**
Sychem Pl. TN12: Five G .1A **30**
Sylvestres TN13: Riv .6D **2**
Symonds La. ME18: Ladd .1K **25**

T

Tainter Rd. TN11: Hdlw .5J **19**
Talbot Pk. TN2: Tun W .4B **34**
Tamar Rd. TN10: Tonb .2K **21**
Tangier La. TN3: Tun W .4J **37**
Tannery Rd. TN9: Tonb .6A **22**
Tannery Rd. Ind. Est. TN9: Tonb .6A **22**
Tanyard La. TN4: S'bgh .7H **27**
Tarland Ho. TN2: Tun W .6B **34**
Tavern Cl. TN15: Bor G .5D **6**
Taylor St. TN4: S'bgh .1H **33**
Tea Gdn. La. TN3: R'hall .1D **36**
Tebbs Way TN15: Igh .2A **12**
Tedder Rd. TN4: Tun W .2K **33**
Teise Cl. TN2: Tun W .7A **34**
Telston La. TN14: Otf .2E **2**
(not continuous)
Terrace, The TN11: Hdlw .6J **19**
TN13: Riv .7D **2**
Teston Rd. ME19: Wro, W Mal .4K **7**
Thames Rd. TN10: Tonb .2K **21**
Theobalds Cl. TN15: Kems'g .3C **4**
Theodore Cl. TN2: Tun W .2C **34**
Thicketts TN13: S'oaks .1J **9**
Third St. TN3: Lang G .6B **32**
Thirlemere Rd. TN4: Tun W .4F **33**
Thomas St. TN4: Tun W .4J **33**
Thomas Wyatt Way TN15: Wro .1D **6**
Thong La. TN15: Bor G .6C **6**
Thorndyke Way TN15: Wro .1D **6**
Thornfield Gdns. TN2: Tun W .4D **34**
Thorpe Av. TN10: Tonb .2A **22**
Three Elm La. TN11: Gold G .2A **24**
TN11: Gold G, Tonb .1F **23**
Three Ways TN9: Tonb .7A **22**
Tilebarn Cnr. TN10: Tonb .3C **22**
Tillmans TN15: Bor G .5E **6**
Tilton Rd. TN15: Bor G .5D **6**
Times Sq. TN1: Tun W .5J **33**
Toby Gdns. TN11: Hdlw .6J **19**
Tockwith Ct. TN13: S'oaks .1J **9**
Tolhurst Rd. TN12: Five G .1A **30**
Tollgate M. TN15: Bor G .5E **6**
Tolsey Mead TN15: Bor G .4E **6**
Tombridge Chambers TN9: Tonb .7K **21**
TONBRIDGE .5K **21**
Tonbridge Angels FC
(Longmead Stadium) .2J **21**
Tonbridge By-Pass TN11: Hild, S'oaks .4B **16**
TN11: Leigh, Hild .1C **20**
TN11: Tonb .1G **27**
Tonbridge Castle .5K **21**
TONBRIDGE COTTAGE HOSPITAL .2A **28**
Tonbridge Ind. Est. TN9: Tonb .6B **22**
Tonbridge Rd. TN2: Pem .7E **28**
TN11: Hdlw .7F **19**
TN11: Hild .1E **20**
TN11: S'brne, Tonb .2A **18**
TN11: Tun W, Pem .7E **28**
TN12: E Peck .3C **24**
TN13: S'oaks .5J **9**
TN15: Plax, Igh .4A **12**
Tonbridge Station (Rail) .6K **21**
Tonbridge Swimming Pool .5K **21**
Torbay TN12: Pad W .2H **25**
Tourist Info. Cen.
Sevenoaks .3J **9**
Tonbridge .5K **21**
Tunbridge Wells .7J **33**
Town Acres TN10: Tonb .3A **22**
Towngate Wood Pk. TN10: Tonb .7C **18**
Town Lock Ho. TN9: Tonb .5A **22**
Town Lock M. TN9: Tonb .5A **22**
Transfesa Rd. TN12: Pad W .7G **25**
Trebilco Cl. TN2: Tun W .2B **34**
Tree La. TN15: Plax .5C **12**
Tree Tops TN9: Tonb .1K **27**
Treetops TN15: Kems'g .2C **4**
Trench Rd. TN10: Tonb .1K **21**
TRENCH WOOD .1K **21**
Trinity Cl. TN2: Tun W .5B **34**
Trinity Theatre & Arts Cen., The .5J **33**
Tristan Gdns. TN4: R'hall .5E **32**
Truro Wlk. TN10: Tonb .2B **22**
Trycewell La. TN15: Igh .6B **6**
Tubs Hill TN13: S'oaks .2H **9**
Tubs Hill Ho. TN13: S'oaks .2G **9**
Tubs Hill Pde. TN13: S'oaks .2G **9**
TUDELEY .7G **23**
Tudeley La. TN9: Tonb .1A **28**
(not continuous)
TN11: Tonb .1A **28**
Tudeley Woods Nature Reserve .5F **29**
Tudor Ct. TN2: Tun W .2G **37**
Tudor Cres. TN14: Otf .1J **3**
Tudor Dr. TN14: Otf .1J **3**
Tulip Tree Cl. TN9: Tonb .7J **21**
Tunbridge Wells Mus. & Art Gallery *.5K 33*
(off Mt. Pleasant Rd.)
TUNBRIDGE WELLS
NUFFIELD HOSPITAL, THE .6A **34**
Tunbridge Wells Sports &
Indoor Tennis Cen. .2H **33**
Tunbridge Wells Station (Rail) .6J **33**
Tunbridge Wells Trade Pk. TN2: Tun W .1B **34**
Tunbridge Wells West Station
Spa Valley Railway .1H **37**
Tunnel Rd. TN1: Tun W .5K **33**
Turner Rd. TN10: Tonb .2C **22**
Turners Gdns. TN13: S'oaks .6J **9**
Tutsham Way TN12: Pad W .2F **31**
Tuxford Rd. TN4: R'hall .4D **32**
Tweed Rd. TN10: Tonb .2A **22**
TWITTON .1E **2**
Twitton La. TN14: Otf .1D **2**
Twitton Mdws. TN14: Otf .1E **2**
Twitton Stream Cotts. TN14: Otf .1E **2**
Twyford Rd. TN11: Hdlw .5H **19**
Tyne Rd. TN10: Tonb .2K **21**

U

UNDERRIVER .1D **16**
Underriver Ho. Rd. TN15: Under .1E **16**
Union Sq. TN4: Tun W .7H **33**
Uplands Cl. TN13: Riv .1F **9**
Uplands Way TN13: Riv .1F **9**
Up. Cumberland Wlk. TN2: Tun W .1J **37**
(not continuous)
Up. Dunstan Rd. TN4: Tun W .3K **33**
Up. Green La. TN11: S'brne .1B **18**
Up. Green Rd. TN11: S'brne .1A **18**
Up. Grosvenor Rd. TN1: Tun W .5J **33**
TN4: Tun W .5J **33**
UPPER HAYESDEN .2E **26**
Up. Haysden La. TN11: Tonb .2F **27**
Upper Nellington TN3: Lang G .5D **32**
Upper Profit TN3: Lang G .6C **32**
Up. Spring La. TN15: Igh .7K **5**
Up. Stephens TN3: Lang G .6C **32**
Upper St. TN4: R'hall .5F **33**
(not continuous)
Upton Quarry TN3: Lang G .6B **32**
Uridge Cres. TN10: Tonb .3A **22**
Uridge Rd. TN10: Tonb .3A **22**

V

Vale Av. TN1: Tun W .6J **33**
TN4: S'bgh .7H **27**
Vale Ct. TN4: S'bgh .6J **27**
Vale Ri. TN9: Tonb .6B **22**
Vale Rd. TN1: Tun W .6J **33**
TN4: S'bgh .6H **27**
TN9: Tonb .6K **21**
Valley Dr. TN11: Hdlw .4K **19**
TN13: S'oaks .4H **9**
Valley Forge Cl. TN10: Tonb .3D **22**
Valley Rd. TN4: R'hall .5E **32**
Valley Vw. TN4: S'bgh .6J **27**
Vaughan Av. TN10: Tonb .1C **22**
Vauxhall Gdns. TN11: Tonb .1A **28**
Vauxhall La. TN4: S'bgh .5H **27**
TN11: Tonb .1A **28**
(not continuous)
Vermont Rd. TN4: R'hall .5E **32**
Vernon Rd. TN1: Tun W .3A **34**
Vestry Cotts. TN14: S'oaks .4J **3**
Vestry Ind. Est. TN14: S'oaks .4J **3**
Vestry Rd. TN14: S'oaks .4H **3**
Vicarage La. TN13: Dun G .4D **2**
Vicarage Rd. TN4: S'bgh .6H **27**
Victoria Gro. TN4: Tun W .6H **33**
Victoria Rd. TN1: Tun W .5K **33**
TN4: S'bgh .7G **27**
TN11: Gold G, Hdlw .2K **23**
TN13: S'oaks .3H **9**
Victory Cotts. TN14: Weald .4J **15**
Vine Av. TN13: S'oaks .2H **9**
Vine Ct. Rd. TN13: S'oaks .2J **9**
Vine Lodge TN13: S'oaks .2J **9**
Vine Lodge Ct. TN13: S'oaks .2J **9**
Vines La. TN11: Hild .5E **16**
Vine, The TN13: S'oaks .2H **9**
Violets, The TN12: Pad W .3G **31**

W

Wagon La. TN12: Pad W .6H **25**
Walker Pl. TN15: Igh .6B **6**
Walks, The TN3: Groom .4C **36**

Wallace Cl. TN2: Tun W 2J 37
Wallers TN3: Speld .2C 32
Wallis Fld. TN3: Groom 6B 36
Walnut Cl. TN12: Pad W 2G 31
Walnut Way TN4: S'bgh 1B 34
Walter's Farm Rd. TN9: Tonb 6A 22
Walton Rd. TN10: Tonb 1D 22
Warberry Pk. Gdns. TN4: Tun W 5G 33
Warham Rd. TN14: Otf 1H 3
Warren Ct. TN13: S'oaks 2J 9
Warren Farm La. TN3: Eri G 6D 36
Warren Ridge TN3: Frant 7A 38
Warren, The TN11: Pens 2A 26
Warrington Rd. TN12: Pad W 2F 31
Warwick Ct. TN13: S'oaks 3H 9
Warwick Pk. TN2: Tun W 7J 33
Warwick Rd. TN1: Tun W 7J 33
Washingstool Hill TN3: Eri G 5E 36
Watercress Cl. TN13: S'oaks 5J 3
Watercress Dr. TN14: S'oaks 5J 3
Waterdown Rd. TN4: Tun W 1F 37
Waterfield TN2: Tun W 3J 37
Waterloo Pl. TN9: Tonb 7K 21
Waterloo Rd. TN9: Tonb 7K 21
Waterman's La. TN12: Pad W, Brenc 4G 31
Water Slippe TN11: Hdlw 5H 19
Waterworks Vs. TN13: S'oaks 4H 9
Watery La. TN15: Seal, Kems'g 7D 4
WATT'S CROSS .7D 16
Waveney Rd. TN10: Tonb 2K 21
Waverley Dr. TN2: Tun W 3D 34
Weald TN14: Weald 4J 15
Weald Ct. TN11: Hild 1F 21
Wealden Cl. TN11: Hild 2G 21
Wealden Pl. TN13: S'oaks 6J 3
Weald Rd. TN13: S'oaks 7H 9
Weald Vw. TN12: Brenc 7K 31
Weald Vw. Rd. TN9: Tonb 1K 27
Weare Rd. TN4: Tun W 1A 34
Weavers La. TN14: S'oaks 6J 3
Webb's All. TN13: S'oaks 3J 9
(not continuous)
Webbs Mdw. TN13: S'oaks 3J 9
Welbeck Av. TN4: Tun W 1A 34
Welland Rd. TN10: Tonb 3K 21
Well Cl. TN11: Leigh 6B 20
Weller Rd. TN4: R'hall 5E 32
Wellmeade Dr. TN13: S'oaks 5H 9
Well Rd. TN14: Otf .1J 3
Wells Cl. TN1: Tun W 6J 33
TN10: Tonb 3B 22
Wells Cotts. TN11: Hild 3F 21
Welton Gdns. TN9: Tonb 1H 27
Westbrook Ter. TN2: Tun W 1B 38
West End TN15: Kems'g 2B 4
Westerham Rd. TN13: Riv 1C 8
TN14: Sund 1B 8
Western Rd. TN1: Tun W 4A 34
TN4: S'bgh 7H 27
TN15: Bor G 5D 6
Westfield TN13: S'oaks 7J 3
W. Heath Cotts. TN13: S'oaks 6H 9
W. Heath La. TN13: S'oaks 6H 9
W. Kent Cold Storage Dpt.
TN14: Dun G 5F 3
W. Park Av. TN4: S'bgh 7H 27
Westrise TN9: Tonb 1J 27
West St. TN15: Wro 1D 6
Westway TN2: Pem 2H 35
Westwood Rd. TN4: R'hall 4D 32
TN12: E Peck 1E 24

Westwood Way TN13: S'oaks 7F 3
Whatcote Cotts. TN15: Bor G 5G 7
Wheatsheaf Way TN10: Tonb 1B 22
Wheelwrights TN15: Plax 6C 12
WHETSTED 7D 24
Whetsted Rd. TN12: Five G 1B 30
Whistler Rd. TN10: Tonb 7B 18
Whitebeam Cl. TN15: Kems'g 2C 4
White Bear Pas. TN1: Tun W 7J 33
Whitebine Gdns. TN12: E Peck 1G 25
White Cott. Rd. TN10: Tonb 1A 22
Whitefield Rd. TN4: Tun W 3J 33
White Friars TN13: S'oaks 5G 9
Whitefriars Wharf TN9: Tonb 6A 22
Whitegate Cl. TN4: Tun W 1J 33
White Hart Cl. TN13: S'oaks 6J 9
White Hart Pde. TN13: Riv 7E 2
White Hart Wood TN13: S'oaks 7J 9
Whitehill TN15: Wro 1F 7
White Ho. La. TN14: S'oaks 1F 15
White Ho. Rd. TN14: S'oaks 1F 15
Whitelake Rd. TN10: Tonb 2A 22
White Lodge TN1: Tun W 5A 34
TN13: S'oaks 6G 9
White Lodge Cl. TN13: S'oaks 1H 9
White Oak Cl. TN9: Tonb 7K 21
Whybourne Crest TN2: Tun W 1A 38
Wickenden Rd. TN13: S'oaks 7J 3
Wickens Cvn. Site TN14: Dun G 4G 3
Wickens Mdw. TN14: Dun G 4F 3
Wickets, The TN14: Weald 3J 15
Wickham Fld. TN14: Otf 1F 3
Wickham Gdns. TN4: R'hall 4F 33
Wickhurst Rd. TN14: Weald 2F 15
Widbury TN3: Lang G 6B 32
WILDERNESSE 7A 4
Wildernesse Av. TN15: Seal, S'oaks 7A 4
Wildernesse Mt. TN13: S'oaks 7K 3
Wildernesse Sports Cen. 6A 4
William Luck Cl. TN12: E Peck 1E 24
William St. TN4: Tun W 4J 33
Willicombe Pk. TN2: Tun W 5B 34
Willow Cres. TN12: Five G 1A 30
Willow La. TN12: Pad W 3K 31
Willow Lea TN10: Tonb 7A 18
Willow Pk. TN14: Otf 2F 3
Willows, The TN15: Igh 6B 6
Willow Tree Rd. TN2: Tun W 1G 37
Willow Wlk. TN2: Tun W 1C 34
Wilman Rd. TN4: Tun W 2J 33
Wilmar Way TN15: Seal 5B 4
Wilson Cl. TN11: Hild 2G 21
Wilson Rd. TN10: Tonb 1C 22
Wiltshire Way TN2: Tun W 2B 34
Winchester Gro. TN13: S'oaks 1H 9
Winchester Rd. TN10: Tonb 2B 22
Wincliff Rd. TN9: Tonb 7K 21
Windmill Cotts. TN14: Weald 4H 15
(off Windmill Rd.)
Windmill Ct. TN2: Tun W 6A 34
(off North St.)
Windmill Hill TN12: Brenc 7H 31
TN15: Wro, Bor G 6H 7
Windmill Pk. TN15: Bor G 5J 7
Windmill Rd. TN13: S'oaks 1H 15
TN14: Weald 4H 15
Windmill St. TN2: Tun W 6A 34
Winfield La. TN15: Bor G 3C 12
WINKHURST GREEN 7B 14
Winkhurst Grn. Rd. TN8: Ide H, Chid 7B 14
Winston Scott Av. TN3: Lang G 5A 32
Witches La. TN13: Riv 7D 2

Withyham Rd. TN3: Withy, Groom 5A 36
Wolseley Rd. TN4: Tun W 2A 34
Woodbury Cl. TN4: Tun W 4J 33
Woodbury Pk. Gdns. TN4: Tun W 4K 33
Woodbury Pk. Rd. TN4: Tun W 4J 33
Wood Dr. TN13: S'oaks 4F 9
Woodfalls Ind. Est. ME18: Ladd 1K 25
Woodfield Av. TN11: Hild 2G 21
Woodfield Rd. TN9: Tonb 7K 21
Woodfields TN13: Riv 7D 2
Woodgate Way TN9: Tonb 7C 22
TN11: Tonb 1B 28
Woodhill Pk. TN2: Pem 3G 35
Woodland Cl. TN4: Tun W 2K 33
Woodland Ri. TN15: Seal, S'oaks 1A 10
Woodland Rd. TN4: Tun W 2A 34
Woodlands TN2: Pem 2K 35
TN12: Pad W 1F 31
Woodlands Cl. TN2: Tun W 5B 34
Woodlands Ct. TN4: S'bgh 6J 27
Woodlands Rd. TN9: Tonb 1J 27
Woodlands, The TN2: Tun W 5A 34
Woodland Way TN4: Bidb 4F 33
Wood Lodge Grange TN13: S'oaks 7J 3
Woodsgate Way TN2: Pem 3F 35
Woodside Cl. TN2: Pem 3J 35
Woodside Rd. TN2: Pem 3J 35
TN4: R'hall 5F 33
TN9: Tonb 1K 27
TN13: S'oaks 1G 9
Wood St. TN1: Tun W 5K 33
Woodview Cres. TN11: Hild 2G 21
Woolley Cl. TN4: S'bgh 7H 27
Woolley Rd. TN4: S'bgh 7H 27
Worships Hill TN13: Riv 1E 8
WROTHAM 1E 6
Wrotham By-Pass TN15: Wro 2E 6
WROTHAM HEATH 4J 7
Wrotham Rd. TN15: Wro, Bor G 5D 6
Wrotham Water Rd. TN15: Tros 1J 7
Wulfred Way TN15: Kems'g 3D 4
Wyatt Cl. TN15: Bor G 5D 6
Wybourne Ri. TN2: Tun W 1K 37
Wye Rd. TN10: Tonb 2K 21
TN15: Bor G 4E 6
Wyndham Av. TN11: Leigh 6B 20
Wyndham Cl. TN11: Leigh 6B 20

Y

Yardley Cl. TN9: Tonb 4B 22
Yardley Pk. Rd. TN9: Tonb 4A 22
Yeoman Gdns. TN12: Pad W 2E 30
Yeoman's Mdws. TN13: S'oaks 4G 9
Yew Tree Cl. TN13: Riv 1D 8
Yew Tree Rd. TN4: S'bgh 1J 33
YOPPS GREEN 4C 12
Yopps Grn. TN15: Plax 4C 12
York Pde. TN10: Tonb 1A 22
York Rd. TN1: Tun W 5J 33
TN10: Tonb 2B 22
YORKS HILL 3B 14
Yorks Hill Rd. TN14: Ide H 2B 14

Z

Zambra Way TN15: Seal 5B 4
Zion St. TN15: Seal 6B 4